The CRADLE, the CROSS and the CROWN

The CRADLE, the CROSS and the CROWN

Sermons for Advent,
Christmas and Epiphany
(Sundays 1-8 in Ordinary Time)

Series A Gospel Texts

GEORGE BASS

C.S.S. Publishing Co., Inc.
Lima, Ohio

THE CRADLE, THE CROSS AND THE CROWN

6826 / ISBN 0-89536-817-X

PRINTED IN U.S.A.

Table of Contents

[1]Common Lectionary (followed by United Methodists, Presbyterians, and others)
[2]Lutheran Lectionary
[3]Roman Catholic Lectionary

Dedicated

to

Willard C. Peterson, M.D.

a caring and dedicated physician

for whom, like God, the very hairs of one's head are numbered

Introduction

The Cradle, the Cross, and the Crown is an attempt to introduce and coordinate the several elements of liturgical preaching to be found in the Christmas cycle. The first, and obvious, ingredient is the Gospel texts that are mostly from Matthew, Series A. The sermons developed from these texts are basically "sermon starters"— ideas, illustrations and stories, theological interpretations, mainly in narrative form. For the most part, the sermons are in an oral style which Clyde Fant (in *Preaching for the Church)* and Lowell Erdahl *(in Preaching for the People)* call "chunks of thought." I simply call this style the "chunk theory" and employ it in my preaching. This type of writing facilitates more direct communication between preacher and people; it helps eliminate the use of a manuscript in the pulpit by changing it into what Robert Hughes, Lutheran Theological Seminary, Philadelphia, calls a preaching "script." It differs from regular literary style in the type and length of sentences, as well as the number and length of paragraphs.

On another level, the preacher must consider that the Christmas cycle — Advent, Christmas, and Epiphany — has three overarching themes — the Cradle, or Incarnation; the Cross, foreshadowing Jesus' death and resurrection; and the Crown, which popularly begins with Jesus' birth and will culminate in the Second Coming, his return and rule. These themes form the framework into which the texts from Matthew, plus a few from John and Luke, are inserted. To make the most of liturgical preaching during the Christmas cycle, the preacher must determine how the theology of Cradle, Cross, and Crown speaks through each text, and what it says in his/her parish setting and the world.

Each of the three seasons of the Christmas cycle reflects, to some degree, the theological motifs of Cradle, Cross, and Crown. Advent articulates several themes related to the Cradle and the Crown, beginning with the Parousia, then the historical coming, his present advent, and the beginning of the Christmas story, as told by both Matthew and Luke. The Cradle — Christmas — always stands before the cross and the empty tomb; Tillich said Jesus was born in a tomb. The Jesus' story moves from Christmas/ Epiphany into manifestation to the world in Jesus' baptism, his miracles and signs (John speaks here), the beginning of his ministry, and his mission to all of humanity. The specific texts assigned to the Sundays of Epiphany are meant to illuminate these themes and expedite the proclamation of the Gospel through them.

Lutherans use the Transfiguration to celebrate the end of the Epiphany season and to serve as a transition to the Easter cycle of Lent and Easter. (It might be better to use the Luke Gospel [9:28-36], which speaks of Jesus ''exodus'' soon to be accomplished through his death in Jerusalem, for all three cycles, in the manner that single sets of lessons are employed for various other festivals of the church year. Lutherans do not observe August 6, the traditional date for the Transfiguration, as a general rule.) The Preachers, especially Roman Catholics who will be celebrating the Eighth Sunday after the Epiphany rather than the Transfiguration at the end of Epiphany this year, need to keep in mind that the shadow of the cross falls over the season from two perspectives — Jesus' birth and baptism, on one hand, and the actual cross event, on the other.

These are the most important things preachers need to consider as they prepare to preach through the Christmas cycle of Advent, Christmas, and Epiphany. They will be preaching liturgically — *The Cradle, the Cross, and the Crown* — if they make use of the whole liturgical context, as well as the appointed texts.

Matthew 24:36-44 (Common) *Advent 1*
Matthew 24:37-44 (Lutheran, Roman Catholic)

A Claim to a Crown

A science-fiction story, *Transit of Earth,* written by Arthur C. Clarke many years ago, was reprinted in *OMNI* magazine in 1984, simply because the basic premise of the story occurred; the story could have happened. The astronomical part of the story is fact; once every century, Mars, Earth, and the Sun are perfectly aligned in a transit that is predictable. The transit took place in 1984, right on time; that part of the story is true, but the rest of it is fiction, which could have happened, but did not. For the fictional story to become reality, there would have to have been an actual landing on Mars by a spaceship inhabited by people whose task, in part, would have been to observe and report on the transit. Such an expedition was prevented by the turmoil of the times and the financial cutbacks on NASA's space program, made necessary by a tired and sick economy.

In Clark's story, a spaceship took off from the earth and landed on Icarus, the small moon which orbits Mars, while the "lander" — Discovery — descended to the surface of the planet with its five-man crew. Discovery's landing turned into tragedy when the perma-frost gave way and the small ship capsized; rescue was impossible. The crew of Discovery was doomed to die on Mars. But they were made of the "right stuff" and decided that the objective of the mission should be completed, if possible; four of the men gave up their supplies of oxygen and died harshly, but quickly, so that the fifth man might record the transit and send his report back to earth.

Once his task was completed, all the last man could do was contemplate death and what would be the easiest way to die. He had three options, he concluded: 1. Simply to allow his oxygen supply to run out and die by asphyxiation; 2. to rip open his space suit and allow the frigid Martian atmosphere to kill him in thirty seconds; or, 3. to take one of the pills in the "med kit" and die in fifteen seconds. His conclusion was: "I will drive (in the Marscar) through that lovely painted landscape . . . And when my oxygen alarm gives its final ping . . ., I'm going to finish in style. As soon as I have difficulty in breathing, I'll get off the Marscar and start walking with a playback unit plugged into my helmet and going full blast. For sheer, triumphant power and glory, there's nothing in music to match the Toccata and Fugue in C Minor . . . I won't have time to hear all of it but that won't matter . . . Johann Sebastian, here I come!" That part of the story might have been, but it didn't take place; the astronomical story did. The *Transit of Earth* not only occurred, but it can be predicted with certainty that it will happen again toward the end of the twenty-first century and once every century, as long as our universe exists.[1]

Jesus was not as accurate as contemporary astronomers when it came to predicting the time of his return to the earth: "This generation will not pass away before these things come to pass." (v. 34) But then he crossed his fingers by saying, "No one knows about that day or hour, not even the angels in heaven, nor the Son, but only the Father." He hasn't returned, as he predicted he would, as yet. But he was right about one thing — that he would die at the hands of the Jewish leaders and rise on the third day. We stake our faith on the validity of the reports of his resurrection passed down to us by the disciples and the evangelists. Could he have been entirely wrong about "the coming of the Son of Man," or could it be simply that God has not determined that the time is ripe for Christ's return and the beginning of his everlasting reign?

That should make us question our predictions — scientific and otherwise — about the threatened end to all life on the earth, shouldn't it? But we know we have good reason to fear the Bomb; it can destroy us — and we had better not forget it. Humanity, not God, by misusing the freedom given by God, might cause the cessation of all life. We have good reason to be afraid. Many people are like the eight-year-old boy, who was carried into the hospital in an episode of *St. Elsewhere,* choking from an acute attack of asthma. It was determined — after tests were completed and he was observed by one of the doctors — that there was no physical cause, no asthma; he was suffering from an unknown psychological phenomenon. As he lay in bed one night, he heard sirens, went to the window, twisted open the Venetian blinds, and then ran out into the empty hallway to find someone. He saw a half-open elevator door, with a warning sign on it, entered it and was later found curled up on the top of the disabled elevator just below floor level. Asked why he was afraid, he replied, "The Bomb." He thought the sirens meant that the end of the world was at hand; he could not be convinced otherwise. Now that the doctor had discovered the cause of his asthma-like condition in his uncontrollable fear of the future, a more complex problem — how to deal with a situation in which we seem to be helpless — had been uncovered and had to be treated. Can predictions of another and worse holocaust than occurred in World War II be allowed to generate an unholy fear in us? Does God have a viable plan in Christ's Second Coming, a plan we can rely on? Does faith in Christ sustain us in the face of a sure and certain death?

If God has given us a gift of grace by postponing Jesus' return until some later time, we had better not spend that time quaking in fear of death or worrying continually about the possible end of humanity and all other life. Jim Klobuchar wrote about the illness and death of a man, Russ Skoe, who lived a rather remarkable kind of life as a pharmacist in northern Minnesota. Despite all the good things he had done, and the whole and healthy person that he was, he was struck down by Lou Gehrig's disease. He and Klobuchar had been on bicycle trips together and, after their last trip, he told the columnist: "You don't do much for yourself or for people around you by brooding over what's ahead . . . But you can't feverishly pack mementos and reunions into every day that's left, afraid that you've forgotten something in trying to relive the part of your life that was good . . . I think if you've lived a life where you've put most of the things in their right order, and mostly if you find some forgiveness in your heart when people louse up or stumble, you feel contentment when you're coming to the end."[2] For Christians, who harbor no fear of death or the future, that might simply suggest a way of "redeeming the time" in which we are living.

To live by faith also means we will do what we can to offset the threat of annihilation of life on earth, first of all, by registering our outrage at the atrocities that war, by itself, inflicts upon people. Not many of us can afford to do what Joan Kroc, the widow of the founder of *McDonald's* fast food chain, did just after Memorial Day had been celebrated in 1985. She bought full pages of newspapers and had the following quote from the late and former President Dwight D. Eisenhower printed beside his picture in his military uniform: "Every gun that is made, every warship launched, every rocket fired signifies, in the final sense, a theft from those who hunger and are not fed, those who are cold and are not clothed. This world in arms is not spending money alone. It is spending the sweat of its laborers, the genius of its scientists, the hopes of its children . . . This is not a way of life at all in any true sense. Under the cloud of threatening war, it is humanity hanging from a cross of iron."[3] Beyond our voiced or written objections to the arms race or the bomb race, it is for us Christians, as the expression of our faith in God, to do the good works of love and mercy — feeding the hungry, caring for the poor, telling people the good news in Jesus Christ — incumbent upon those who believe Jesus is the living Lord who will come again.

Some time ago, my wife and I were in the Imprimatur Gallery, in St. Paul, and were attracted to a small, faceless sculpture, handless arms upraised, back gracefully curved, which was titled, "Free Spirit;" it was the work of Brother Jerome Cox. On the other side of the room, also on the wall, we discovered a crucifix done in exactly the same style, but with a difference. This figure had a face, hands, and could be identified as the Risen Lord, who seemed to be bursting forth from the tomb. He has conquered the cross and death, and it is obvious he is the reason for the "Free Spirit," the freeing of humanity from the fear of sin and death so people might become all God intends them to be and live lives pleasing to him and profitable to the whole human race. The young man in charge of the gallery told us: "It (the Christ figure) was in the basement, overlooked in the unpacking after we moved here. It fell out of a box that we were moving one day." And then they realized what they had, cleaned and polished it, and hung it on the wall for all to see. That combination of sculptures is a reminder of the freedom, to live and serve fearlessly and faithfully, that the risen Christ gives to us all.[4]

Before he died, Jesus predicted, "As were the days of Noah, so will be the coming of the Son of Man." The resurrection of the Lord affirmed the truth of that prediction, even if Jesus seemed to be wrong about its proximity. But he will return — unexpectedly, suddenly — when God is good and ready. In the meantime, we may live hopefully and confidently the life our Lord has given to us, doing works of faith and love that are pleasing to him. Perhaps we may even learn to pray the prayer of the first Christians: "Come, Lord Jesus! Come, quickly!" When he does return, at last, he will claim his crown as Lord of all.

A Call for a Change in Lifestyle

At the mention of the name, John the Baptizer, I immediately think of two churches that are thousands of miles apart. One is only eighty-five miles from my home, the Benedictine abbey church of St. John the Baptist on the campus of St. John's University, Collegeville, Minnesota. The other church is thousands of miles away, just outside of Florence, Italy, at the confluence of two superhighways. Each features visual images of John the Baptizer. The church in Italy pictures the life and death of John on great bronze "book pages" that line the walls of a corridor in that building. The other, in Minnesota, is striking, partly because sculpture of the Baptizer is done in black, so that John becomes a rather roughly-hewn, stark, and commanding figure, who stands at the side of the font in the atrium, preaching silently to the people who pass by the font on their way into the nave of the church.[5]

On this Sunday in Advent, I would like to place a statue of John and a tape recorder on which his basic message, "Repent, for the kingdom of heaven is at hand," had been recorded, in every Christian church, playing that message before each mass or service. All of the people would be confronted with John's prediction, too, "I baptize you with water for repentance, but he who is mightier than I, whose sandals I am not worthy to carry; he will baptize you with the Holy Spirit and with fire." The message would be played over and over, not only as people entered the church, but as they left it, as well. I believe people would hear and comprehend this part of the Advent message and, perhaps, never forget it.

But can you imagine what would happen in our time, if preachers dared to articulate the rest of John's message? Suppose people were addressed in the same terms that John used in preaching to the Pharisees and Sadducees of his day: "You brood of vipers! Who warned you to flee from the wrath to come? Bear fruit that fits repentance, and do not presume to say to yourselves, 'We have Abraham as our father'; for I tell you, God is able from these stones to raise up children to Abraham. Even now the axe is laid to the root of the trees; every tree therefore that does not bear good fruit is cut down and thrown into the fire . . . His winnowing fork is in his hand, and he will clear his threshing floor and gather his wheat into the granary, but the chaff he will burn with unquenchable fire." There's not much good news in that message, is there, especially for people who are self-satisfied and close-minded where God is concerned. John sounds too much like a "fire and brimstone" evangelist, who belongs to another age, doesn't he? Can his message be for us — here and now?

Sometimes it takes a radical idea or action to get the attention of people and make them listen, think, and go into action. John was faced with an extraordinarily difficult task. He saw himself as, "The voice of one crying in the wilderness: Prepare the way of the Lord, make his paths straight." He was to herald the coming of the Messiah to people who claimed they were awaiting his coming, but who — like us — only wanted him to come on their terms. Religious leaders heard his message and quickly rejected it, immediately beginning to plan and plot how they might silence him or get rid of him entirely. The common people heard him and must have understood what he was preaching about, "Repent, for the kingdom is at hand . . . Be baptized and saved." But what does this have to do with us?

For one thing, we have been baptized, most of us in our infancy, and we have been Christians all of our lives. But this does not mean we are sinless and have no need of repentance. Luther labeled us both saints and sinners, reminding us it is necessary to repent daily and relive our baptismal covenant of dying and rising with Christ every day of our lives. Repentance is an act of dying, and it is necessary to genuine Christianity. It seems to me one of the great losses of Protestantism is the neglect of signing oneself with water "in remembrance of our death in baptism" as one enters the church. That's what St. John's John the Baptizer reminds me to do.

Recently, I was in the home of a former member of a parish I served. He and his wife are retired and have just moved from a lovely home into a condominium. They took me on a tour of their new living quarters, dominated by books in every room, even over the doors, along with a grand piano that nearly fills up one of the rooms. Their home is furnished with lovely Pennsylvania Dutch antiques, including a stiking canopy bed in their bedroom. But it was a prie-dieu in the bedroom that really caught my attention, upholstered in hand-woven red fabric that clearly showed the imprint of knees on it, as testimony to the devotional life of these people. But I wonder if we do not equally need a simple bowl of water at our bedside into which we might dip our finger tips when we get up and when we go to bed, making the sign of the cross "In the name of the Father, Son, and Holy Spirit" as an act of devotion, an act of repentance and death, and in assurance that our sins have been forgiven and heaven is our final destiny.

Dying in baptism comes no more easily than physical death; we avoid acts of penitence and contrition like a plague. Yet spiritual death is necessary to new life, according to John, Jesus, Paul, and the other writers of the New Testament. New life of any kind almost always is preceded by some, often radical, kind of death. People who abuse drugs and alcohol have to learn that before they can be helped. Over thirty years ago, I wrote a master's thesis on "A Christian Approach to Alcoholism."[6] I came to the conclusion that the most Christian approach to addressing the problem and helping alcoholics was, at that time, Alcoholics Anonymous. The point is not that it preaches the Gospel directly to people, but it calls for a kind of spiritual death in the Fifth Step, an admission of one's inability to free oneself from addiction to alcohol or drugs, plus the necessity to realize that a recovering alcoholic can only live one day at a time. That is very close to Luther's insistence that everybody, not just alcoholics or other drug abusers, has to die daily in order to live a new life. The problem is that members of AA more heartily embrace this theological truth than most Christians do. So John really is speaking to you and me when he says, "Repent, (and be baptized), for the kingdom of heaven is at hand.

If Advent contains a call to repentance (and a sort of death) on the one hand, it is also a reminder that we Christians are to live a new kind of life every day. Repentance is really changing one's lifestyle, so the concerns and the commands of Christ come above everything else we do or think. Repentance is really living for Christ, living out the life Christ has given us rather than living for ourselves.

Our life-styles should declare, "He's worth it!" instead of "I'm worth it!" or "I deserve it (the good life)." Christ gives us a life to live; he does not threaten to take it away from us. One of my students, now the Rev. Zane Wilson, told an unforgettable, true story in a chapel sermon. In his first career as a policeman, he had the responsiblity of conducting on the job training of rookie officers. One day, as he was breaking in a new recruit, they received a message that a man was threatening to kill himself. He had a gun and would allow no one near him. They answered the call and Zane gave the rookie careful instructions before they got to the address: "Be calm. Keep your gun holstered. Don't do anything to agitate him." When they got to the home of the potential suicide, the rookie policeman jumped out of the car, drew his gun, ran up to the door, threw it open, dashed into the house right to the man with the gun held to his head, pointed his pistol at the man, and shouted, "Drop it, or I'll blow your head off." The man was so startled that he did drop the gun, but the recruit had violated procedures and could have caused the man to pull the trigger and kill himself. Christ, we may be assured, has come to give us life and to give it abundantly, but it takes a kind of death to turn us around so we might live out our lives on earth in faith, love, and service to God and humanity.

John's self-identification with Isaiah's "Prepare the way of the Lord, make his paths straight" sharpens the focus of how we might embrace a life-style that is pleasing to Jesus Christ. A colleague, Prof. James Burtness, tells how his eighty-three-year-old mother "prepares the way for the Lord." The setting is the town K-Mart store in southern Illinois and, he says: "My mother is there, just picking up a few things. When the blue light special is announced, she moves, fast. At the checkout counter she stands in line in front of the young boy. 'What did you get? I got a watch for $5.98 — including the battery.' It's very nice, very genuine. She's a nice woman and she likes people. She's also a Christian. Somewhere along the line, she asks the boy where he goes to Sunday school. He doesn't go. 'Really? Oh, I think you'd like it. Could I call your mother and see if I can pick you up? We have a choir, too. The kids have a lot of fun.' My mother calls his mother. No problem. So every Sunday my eighty-three-year-old mother is picking up ten-year-old James for Sunday school and choir. His sister asks if she can come, too. Then there is a concert, and the mother wants to come to hear the children's choir. There is no father in this family, but the mother and the two children pile into my mother's 73 Pontiac for Sunday school and church. James has a birthday party, and there's my mother, guest of honor, with a funny hat and a balloon, along with eight ten-year-olds. In time, it is discovered that there are some roots in the local Methodist congregation. Contacts are made, introductions, and the mother and her children are firmly established in that congregation. Meanwhile, my mother is back at the K-Mart, and at the drug store, and on her walks around her apartment, and stories similar to the one I've just told you go on and on and on."[7] Isn't that one way of preparing the way for the Lord's coming? And isn't that a type of life-style that is pleasing to Jesus Christ?

That's what is expected of us, when we listen to John the Baptizer in Advent. "Repent, for the kingdom of heaven is at hand . . . Prepare the way of the Lord, make his paths straight."

A Desperate Question

John the Baptizer was in trouble, and not knowing exactly what his fate would be, he suspected the worst. He was in for a long and uncomfortable imprisonment, at best, and he could expect to be executed, at worst. John was soon to lose his head, as you and I know very well, so Herod could save face. He knew he was in trouble. For some unexplained reason, he rather suddenly and unexpectantedly, after reports that his ministry was devoted to preparing the way of the Lord, became uncertain about Jesus' identity. For the second time — this time from jail — he sent disciples to Jesus with a knotty question for the person he believed to be the Messiah.

On this occasion, John's disciples were instructed to ask Jesus about his identity, not about matters like eating and drinking on the Sabbath. There's a measure of quiet desperation in the question they had been instructed to ask: "Are you he who is to come, or shall we look for another?" He had to have an answer to that perplexing problem and he had to have it soon; his fate depended on it, to some degree. Apparently, he was bothered by the reports that filtered down to him about the kind of ministry Jesus was engaged in. The training mission, on which Jesus had sent the twelve, seems to have precipitated a kind of personal crisis causing him to doubt that Jesus was the long-expected Messiah, and the matter had to be settled before it was too late. He must have wanted to die in peace; he had to have an answer to his question.

In the movie, *Desperately Seeking Susan,* it is not really Susan, a veritable free spirit, who is being sought by her friends and lovers, but Roberta who is doing the desperate seeking. Roberta is the wife of a very successful spa and tub salesman. She lives in a luxurious apartment house in New York City, and has about everything anyone could desire. But her life is empty; it has no meaning, no purpose, and, to make matters worse, she gradually comes to the realization that her husband is in love with himself, not with her. His greatest pleasure is to watch himself in the commercials he has made for his product. Roberta manages to change places with the real Susan, and in the process, she discovers a man who really loves her. When Susan, later in the story visits Roberta's apartment, she opens the drawer in the bedside table and takes out some of the books that Roberta reads: *I'M OK, YOU'RE OK,* a "how to get more out of sex" book, and one on "how to communicate." It becomes clear that Roberta is desperately searching for herself, her own identity, not simply for a tawdry affair with a temporary lover. She has to have an answer to a "Who am I?" question, such as many people ask today. The movie might very well have had a title like, "The Desperate Search of Roberta." The final act of lovelessness by her husband, Gary, occurs when he discovers her as part of an act in a sleezy Magic Club and gives her an ultimatum: "I'll give you five minutes, and then I'll leave." He does, and without intending to, enables her to make her decision to return to Desi, the man who loves her and offers a totally different kind of life than she had known before. Her decision meant renunciation of luxuries and the kind of temporal pleasures she had with Gary — the cause of her desperate search and questions — and the acceptance of a different, yet simpler and more satisfying, life-style with Desi.[8]

That kind of a desperate search, with its haunting questions about personal identity, which have given rise to all sorts of pop psychology, surely is very important, but is not the ultimate quest in life. It is the person of Jesus — who he really is — that ought to raise the paramount questions for us. And it is a positive answer to that same question which John asked, "Are you the one,or shall we look for another?" which gives ultimate meaning to our lives and enables us to live without fear and anxiety. A few days ago, I was tuning my radio and happened to hear the name John Lewis, along with "missionary pilot in Zaire, Africa," so I listened and heard John speak. He told a story about an encounter with death that happened recently on a river in Zaire. John's mother. who is our next-door neighbor, had told the story to my wife, and now I heard him tell it. His wife's parents were visiting John and his family in Africa and he wanted to show them the wildlife of the country; John, his wife, Anita, and their children, her parents, and a native got into a small boat and went out on a muddy river to look for crocodiles. Someone spotted a hippo and everyone went to one side of the boat to look; the boat capsized and they were all thrown into the water. Only their two small children had life vests; her parents could not swim. They all splashed around desperately in the water, but somehow John and Anita managed to get everyone onto the overturned boat as it was swept down the river. They were absolutely helpless for about twenty minutes, and then they spotted a fisherman in a dugout canoe and called to him; he heard and came to their rescue. Along with another fisherman, he managed to get the whole party to shore, where they were ultimately found and taken back to civilization. John said he was positive God was responsible for their rescue, and he is probably right; it could have been their faith in the living Lord that enabled John and Anita to remain calm in those minutes after the boat overturned. Their faith in the risen Christ banished all fear of death so they could stare into the very mouth of death and defeat it because they knew Christ was with them. They know Jesus is "the One" and they don't have to seek another for faith and satisfaction. In a way, they were better off than was John the Baptizer when he faced death in prison.[9]

Jesus didn't give John a straight answer; he simply told John's disciples, "Go and tell John what you hear and see: the blind receive their sight and the lame walk, lepers are cleansed and the deaf hear, and the dead are raised up, and the poor have good news preached to them. And blessed is he who takes no offense at me." That's a very strange answer when we put it over against Jesus' encounter with Nicodemus in John's Gospel. Nicodemus discovered that flattery would get him nothing when he addressed Jesus, "Teacher I know you are a man come from God, for no one could do the things you do unless God were with him." Jesus immediately shot him down, "you must be born anew if you would even see the kingdom of heaven." Jesus wouldn't allow Nicodemus to identify him simply as a teacher or a miracle worker; he wanted him to see who he really was and that's why he said for a second time, "Unless a man is born anew, he cannot enter the kingdom of heaven." Jesus would not allow himself to be classified as another of the Mediterranean magicians who was able to do all sorts of magic tricks with and upon the sick and the handicapped. Morton Smith, in his book, *Jesus the Magician,* writes: "Jesus the magician was the figure seen by most ancient opponents of Jesus. Jesus the Son of God was the figure seen by that part of his followers that eventually triumphed;

the real Jesus was the man whose words and actions gave rise to these contradictory interpretations." Smith came to the conclusion that "the real Jesus was a magician, nothing more — not quite as good as Appolonius who vanished from Domitian's Roman court and escaped execution." Jesus didn't know a trick by which he could make himself slip out of Pilate's judgment hall and, accordingly, was condemned to death on a cross.[10]

But Jesus was willing to take the risk of John's misinterpreting his answer to John's disciples, and seeing Jesus as a miracle worker or a magician, or simply as another religious teacher. He was positive John would understand that his "go and tell John" answer spelled out the fulfillment of the Scriptures about what sort of things the Messiah would do when he came to earth. Jesus knew he would recognize him as Messiah from the works he was able to do, and he was willing to run that risk. His mission to the world of people was to become totally involved in human life and affairs; that's what his advent and his incarnation really mean — God cares and loves us enough to be with us in all we do, all we endure and suffer in this life. When former President Jimmy Carter participated in the renovation of some slum housing in New York City, a black man who lived there said, "When you come down to the muscle, then you show you care." That's all he offered John in Herod's prison as he awaited his fate — but that, obviously, was enough; it quieted his doubts, put down his fears, and gave him the courage to face whatever Herod would do to him.

That is the Christ we need, if there is to be any semblance of peace and comfort in our lives, the absence of unreasonable fear, and the courage we need to face life and, even, death. Many people seem to be looking for a Christ who will perform the necessary, as well as the wished for, miracles in their lives and, in the process, settle for something less than "the One who is to come." Headlines in our newspaper recently read: "(Doug) Henning concentrating on small wonders." The feature article told how and why he is the premiere magician today and the sub-headline read: "Henning: His first trick was making pet turtle disappear."[11] Jesus' first miracle was turning water into wine, but the greatest wonder is he gives us himself and the blessing of his presence in all that we do. And, as it was for John, so it is with us: "And blessed is he who takes no offense at me"— he gives us himself and the promise of heaven's richest blessings, life with him in the age yet to come. When we know that, we not only may face up to all life has to offer, but we are released from our bondage to self so we might enter fully into his mission here on earth.

Some time ago, I met a young woman pastor from Washington, D.C., at a Preaching From Commitment seminar in Maryland. She certainly preached her sermon in the seminar from a position of positive commitment to Christ. The "commitment" part of her ministry came out in conversations, rather than directly in her preaching. She is pastor of an inner-city church and lives, with her husband and two children, right in the neighborhood where the church is located. It is not an easy existence for them; most of their neighbors have accepted them, but still their home was broken into and robbed four times in less than six months. After the third robbery, her husband cemented up an under-the-porch basement window, by which the thieves gained entry to the house. When the thieves were thwarted on their fourth attempt to enter the house, they went up to the roof, chopped a hole in it, and entered through the main bedroom. "As soon as we went into the house," the pastor said, "we knew we had been robbed again. And when I went into the bedroom and discovered how they had gotten in, I felt that I had been violated and raped. That just seemed too much to take." But she intends to stay there, in the middle of Washington, D.C., and minister and preach to people who need Jesus just as much as she does. She knows Christ is the One, and she doesn't have to search desperately for another Savior.

Is Christ the One sent by God to be with us and to save us from sin and the fear of death? Maybe if we pay attention to his words and deeds, in the light of his life, death, and resurrection, we will find an answer — as John the Baptizer did — that satisfies our souls.

Matthew 1:18-25 (C, L)
Matthew 1:18-24 (RC)

Joseph's Dream

God was working overtime when he visited Joseph, Mary's fiance, in a fantastic dream shortly before the two of them were to be married. An angel — it must have been Gabriel — appeared in his dream and told him to go ahead with the marriage, despite the fact Mary was pregnant. That would make a story in itself; who would think of marrying someone who was going to deliver a child fathered by another person, especially in those times and that kind of society? But this is not the beginning of the story.

Gabriel's work, in the Christian story, begins with his appearance to Zechariah, the father of John the Baptizer, when he was serving in the Temple. He announced the impending pregnancy of Elizabeth and described the mission of the child who was to be born and named John, but Zechariah found all of this too much to believe. Oddly enough, when Joseph merely had a dream in which an angel spoke to him, he believed. Had he heard about Zechariah? He probably knew nothing about that incident, but Mary must have told him her story about Gabriel's appearance to her and his incredible news; Mary was to be the mother of the long-awaited Messiah! Gabriel didn't even make a personal visit to Joseph when he was awake, but simply appeared to him in a dream.

And what a dream that must have been! Joseph must have awakened with a start, perhaps hoping the dream would go away. When it didn't, he surely had some immediate reactions to it. Could he trust the reality of it, or was it merely a dream? And what about the "virgin Mary" part of the announcement? Why should he believe such an implausible tale? Should he go ahead with the marriage, stand by Mary at the birth of the child, and then give the name

Jesus — God with us — to the child?

There is no doubt the dream experience convinced Joseph Mary's story was true. She couldn't concoct a tale like that. She had to be intelligent enough to realize such a story was too much for people to accept; no one would believe her — except, and only after his dream-visitation, Joseph. Can you imagine what her reaction must have been when Joseph told her he would go through with their plans for the wedding? The poet could have been speaking for her, instead of Saul Kane, when he wrote:

I did not think, I did not strive,
A deep peace burned in me alive.
The bolted door had broken in,
I knew that I was done with sin.
I felt that Christ had given me birth
To brother all the souls on earth.
I thought all earthly creatures knelt
With rapture at the joy I felt.[12]

Joseph believed her and he would marry her! Her heart must have been overflowing with love and gratitude when Joseph told her the wedding was still on. Joseph's dream of an angel's visit was as real to him as was Gabriel's appearance to Mary. And he obeyed the directions which the angel gave to him and married Mary! Their marriage must have been interesting, but neither Matthew nor Luke gives any account of it; they only tell us that Mary carried Jesus until it was time for his birth, and they didn't consummate the marriage until after Jesus was born.

But surely Joseph must have had some thoughts about this child who was to be born. What would he be like, this child of God through the Holy Spirit? Would he be fully human or, perhaps, super-human? At least, people in this day and age, when fertility drugs can produce septuplets, would have such concerns about the normality of the child to be born. Ray Bradbury once wrote a story that he called "Tomorrow's Child." Peter Horn took his wife to a hospital in a helicopter, and then awaited the birth of his son. He was on his third highball when the physician, Dr. Wolcott, came into the waiting room, looking "like a man who has seen death." "She's dead," Peter responded. "No," said Wolcott, "No, no, she's fine. It's the baby." "The baby's dead, then." "The baby's alive, too, but — drink the rest of that drink and come along after me," directed the doctor. "Something's happened." It seemed the entire hospital staff was out in the corridors, whispering to each other; Peter became "quite ill." When he and the doctor entered a small room, a crowd of people was looking down at a low table and at what was on it — "a small Blue Pyramid."

Someone said, "It weighs seven pounds, eight ounces." Peter thought it was an April Fool joke, but the doctor insisted, "This is your child. Understand that, Mr. Horn." "No, no, it's not. (His mind wouldn't touch the thing.) It's a nightmare. Destroy it!"

But the doctor said, "You can't kill a human being." "Human?" Horn blinked tears. "That's not human! That's a crime against God!" But the doctor explained that the child was not a mutant, nor a freak, nor sick: "The child was somehow affected by the birth pressure. There was a dimensional disstructure caused by the simultaneous short-circuitings and malfunctionings of the new birth and hypnosis machines. Well, anyway," the doctor ended lamely, "your baby was born into another dimension . . . (and) because it was born into another dimension it has an alien shape to us. Our eyes, adjusted to a three-dimensional concept, cannot recognize it as a baby. But it is . . . (and) it is your child."[13] That kind of child would just not do. God had to produce, through this mystical union of Mary and the Holy Spirit, a child who would be normal and healthy, a baby who was just like every other normal child, as the Son of God. The Christ, born two thousand years ago, was to be a true and genuine "Tomorrow's Child" for all time and all people. "The Word became flesh and dwelt among us" — that's incarnation.

Joseph affirmed Mary's experience with Gabriel in an kind of "So be it. Let God do his miracle. We will abide by it." They were probably more aware than we are that every birth is a miracle wrought by God. God, in a sense, is the ultimate magician, continuing to work his miracles of creation in our world. Human magicians are best at making things disappear and, sometimes, reappear. But they cannot do what God has done and is doing in his creation. Doug Henning, for example, began by making his pet turtle disappear, "then he moved on to his hamster, a snake — he had to abandon that because squeamish onlookers would scream and run away — doves, rabbits and the family poodle. Of course, that was just the start. He eventually 'graduated' to a 259-pound lion, a 500-pound Bengal tiger and, finally, to a 4-ton elephant."[14] Magicians are experts at making things disappear, but they could not work a miracle (nor can the greatest scientists, who are the real magicians of our age) like the one God did through the Holy Spirit and the Virgin Mary. Joseph accepted it for what it was and obeyed the command of the angel.

God got on with his miracle. He did something as fantastic for that age as some of the proposals for the future by contemporary scientists. Edward Regis, Jr., in an article, "Mother Sun," seems to be fantasizing when he looks ahead to conditions in this solar system in A.D. 2600. He believes, with some other scientists, that the human race will inhabit most of the planets and asteroids of the system in 600 years: "But there's a catch. Although there are hundreds of billions of people spread out from one end of the solar system to the other, planetary materials are nearing exhaustion. A solar-wide materials crisis looms, something that will make the earthside 'energy crunch' of the 1970's seem just like a ripple." Regis writes about David R. Criswell, who "walks the earth just like the rest of us. But for most of us, that's where the similarity ends, for Criswell spends a lot of time thinking on immense spatiotemporal scales. He has patent applications pending for lunar power stations . . . (and) is president of his own space applications company." Criswell even has a plan to meet the projected materials crisis of A.D. 2600; he believes that human beings can take the sun apart through the use of particle accelerators, thereby providing a virtually inexhaustible source of energy and materials to support human life in this universe. Two thousand years ago, the announcement of a "virgin birth" must have been just as incredible as Criswell's Plan for "Mother Sun." But through God-given faith, Joseph was able to accept the promised miracle and act accordingly on it.

The comfort and hope for us, in all of this, is simply that we know we have a mighty and powerful God, who is not only interested in our welfare, but is able to do something about our eternal predicament — sin and death — through Jesus Christ. We know Jesus is really with us, as his name suggests, entering into everything we experience and sharing all of life with us. According to an ancient legend, "One of Francis of Assisi's disciples found his shivering master walking naked one night in the heart of winter. 'Why do you go naked in such cold, Father Francis?' he said to him in astonishment. 'Because, my brother, thousands upon thousands of brothers and sisters are cold at this moment. I have no blankets to give them to make them warm, so I join them in their coldness'."

Jesus not only joins us, coming into the world as naked as any other child, but he brought us and gives to us the very blessings of God the Father to minister to us and meet our deepest needs.

Have you ever wondered what might have happnened if Joseph had reacted to the angel's visit as "only a dream"? But it was a dream and more; he had a visit from God, and that was as real to him as were the dreams the other Joseph had to deal with, long before his time. So he did what God wanted him to do. Isn't there a lesson in all of that for us, too, as we prepare to celebrate the birth of Jesus, our Savior and Lord?

Luke 2:1-20 (Common, Lutheran)
Luke 2:1-14 (Roman Catholic)

The Nativity of our Lord
(Christmas Eve/Christmas Day)

A Manger is Christ's Cradle

Christ is born! A rough manger is his cradle. We have a reason for rejoicing, even today, in a world that makes us ponder the fate of the whole human race, perhaps of all life on the earth. The story of the birth of Christ unfolds, according to St. Luke, much like a play in four acts, therein revealing our cause for celebration of Christ's birth at his cradle in Bethlehem.

The first act has to do with the journey Mary and Joseph had to make from Nazareth to Bethlehem. About all we know of the journey is it was something like eighty miles, and it would take, by foot or donkey, several days to complete. As I write this, neighbors of mine have just departed for Lancaster, Pennsylvania; their trip is about a thousand miles farther than that which the expectant parents had to make years ago. They left in a rather plush van-camper yesterday afternoon; they will be in Lancaster sometime this afternoon, simply because they have three people to share the driving and they will not stop overnight. My neighbors will be in Lancaster in less than twenty-four hours from the time they started out from St. Paul, Minnesota. Even with a fifty-five mile per hour speed limit, they can make this trip with relative ease and without fear of being attacked, beaten, or robbed on the highway. That's a far cry from the kind of travel people had to endure at the beginning of the Christian era. Mary had no upholstered chair to rest in on the way to Bethlehem; she probably had to walk a good portion of the way. And that might not have been all bad, because it might have helped her gain strength for the delivery of the baby. But they could not dally around on the journey, because her baby was due to arrive any day.

But, despite the fact that neither Matthew nor Luke gives us any details of the journey of the young man and woman, it certainly was not an easy trip. The ruling Romans made it necessary by decreeing one of their every-so-often tax registration periods; Joseph had to be in Bethlehem by a certain date, which probably put some additional pressure on them as they traveled. So they made the trip, probably in a little caravan of people going to Jerusalem, or beyond, for companionship and protection. It was much safer, in those days, to travel in groups than it was to make solitary journeys. The trip must have been uneventful, otherwise some of the details would have been remembered and written down as part of the story. That's the first act in the story about the birth of Jesus Christ.

They apparently had no problems until they reached Bethlehem and were unable to find a place to stay. Odd that such a thing should happen. After all, Joseph was from Bethlehem; at least, it was his ancestral home and he should have been familiar with all aspects of life there. Not very much would change in a matter of a couple of decades or even a longer period of time; some things, some towns never seem to change, and so it should have been with Bethlehem. Joseph should have known how many inns there were and he should have made his plans accordingly, but he didn't. The public inn or inns had been occupied before they started looking for shelter. And where were his relatives? Surely, there must have been someone who knew him and could have helped them out. I suspect Joseph panicked a bit when he discovered that "there was no room for them in the inn."

Some years ago, my wife and I and our two children were driving from Spain through southern France on our way to Italy. We had made no reservations for this part of our journey, despite the fact that we were traveling in the European vacation month of August. We decided we should stay in Nice and, after we got into the city, we parked our car and my wife and I set out to find two rooms for the night. Every room in Nice seemed to have been booked in advance; no one could even suggest where we might find space. Our search appeared to be hopeless, but we didn't want to go back and tell the children that we had to drive on in approaching darkness until we found a place to spend the night. Besides, we wanted to spend part of a day in this lovely resort city, so we continued to look. The twenty-second place where we stopped just happened to have space for us — on the ground floor. Gratefully, we took it, and we weren't even perturbed when we discovered, upon awakening the next morning, that people were eating breakfast in the courtyard right outside of our bedroom windows. We had an idea, I now realize, of how Jospeh must havc felt when he and Mary arrived in Bethlehem that day and found all of the accommodations taken. At least, we could have slept in the car and, more importantly, my wife wasn't expecting the birth of a baby. Mary was — immanently — and they had no place to stay.

The innkeeper, at least, was a compassionate man. He couldn't give them space in the inn, but he couldn't simply turn them away, either. He might have said, "Spend the night in the manger; there's plenty of clean, fresh hay there to make a bed. Some of my guests are leaving tomorrow and, I promise you, I'll see that you get their room when it is prepared." So with no other option open to them, Mary and Joseph went out to the cave-like stable and made a bed for themselves among the animals. But sleep was not to be theirs that night, for Mary soon was in hard labor and, before long, gave birth to her first-born son, Jesus, snd laid him in the manger. That's the end of the second part of the drama.

Now the whole story begins to get more complicated and more enthralling. Some very strange things began to happen outside of Bethlehem where shepherds were standing night watch over their flocks. Have you ever seen the Northern Lights as nature puts on a "light" show of her own? It is something to be remembered, as waves of light pulsate across the night sky. Occasionally, and if one is far enough away from the city lights, the entire heavens seem to light up. Something similar happened that night long ago, as one poet put it:

And what of the night, was the moon aglow
Was the galaxy veiled or fair?
Only the men know of that sky long ago,
The gleam of a star was there.[16]

If it were a single star putting on the spectacular show that night, it must have been so bright it lighted up the entire sky. The shepherds, who were used to seeing all sorts of strange things at night, had never seen anything like it. And, with good reason, they were afraid. Who wouldn't be? It must have seemed to them that something terrible was about to happen. They soon found out they had nothing to fear, because they were the first ones to hear the "good news" about the birth of the Savior.

Without the presence of the angels and their announcement, the shepherds might never have known what they had seen was "the glory of the Lord," let alone the most momentous event in the history of humanity had happened not far from where they were. Was it that busy angel, Gabriel, who spoke to them: "Be not afraid; for behold, I bring you good news of a great joy which shall be to all the people; for to you is born this day in the city of David a Savior, who is Christ the Lord. And this will be a sign for you: you will find the babe wrapped in swaddling cloths and lying in a manger." They immediately knew what they were to do; the angel made that very clear to them. They were not simply spectators at a cosmic spectacular that night, but theirs, appropriately, was the privilege of being the first humans to pay homage to the new-born Messiah. This newly-born child would be known as the Good Shepherd and, after he was grown up, he would lay down his very life for the sheep — for all people. The shepherds knew what they were to do — get to Bethlehem as rapidly as they could to see this holy child the angel had told them about. Suddenly, all the angels began to sing:

Glory to God in the highest,
and on earth, peace among men with
whom he is pleased!

And as heaven and earth seemed to reverberate to their glorious song of praise, the third act came to an end.

So the shepherds made their way to Bethlehem and found the manger where Jesus had been born, as quickly as they could. What they did when they saw the infant child is not known or, at least, never got into the story. But the result of that visit to the manger, connected as it was to the strange and marvelous events which took place out in the fields that night, was recorded; they immediately went out to tell people about this wonderful thing that had happened. They were the first missionaries, and they told the whole story as it happened to them and, especially, as it pertained to the good news, the birth of Jesus the Savior. Mary, who along with Joseph, heard the fantastic story of the shepherds, "pondered all these things in her heart." She knew it was as Gabriel had told her nine months earlier, that she was indeed blessed by God who had chosen her to be mother of the Son of God. Years later, she would learn how much heartache that fact would bring her, but for this night, she had a reason to rejoice and, with Joseph, she did just that. Jesus the Savior is born. It is almost the end of the fourth act, but not quite.

This is where we come in. We have heard the beautiful story and we ponder its meaning in our hearts. We have sung the angels' song this night, we go to his Table, remembering his birth in that manger-cradle, to greet him whom we know as Lord. And Christ himself, the crucified and risen One, the Savior of the world, comes to us with the gift of himself. We join the shepherds, as we leave his Table, and go out to tell the world the good news — Christ is born, the Savior of us all! And that, indeed, is a reason for rejoicing.

Matthew 2:13-15, 19-23

Christmas 1 (C, L)
Holy Family (RC)

Deliverance by a Dream

It is a scene burned into my memory; I remember the death of the Cambodian child as though it had just happened. My granddaughter and I had just finished watching Cookie Monster do his stuff on *Sesame Street,* and the national news came on. My granddaughter immediately left, but another took her place, not on my lap, but on the television screen. I was whisked off to a refugee camp in Cambodia and, right before my eyes, a refugee mother began to mourn the death of her baby, who had just died. She invaded my den, wailed and wept in my presence, and I felt that the child had just died in the den.[17] Indeed, as we have been it seeing it happen all over the world, "Rachel is weeping for her children and will not be comforted."

It might have been Mary weeping for her son, Jesus, if Herod had been successful in his attempt to kill the baby. But Jesus was delivered from death by two dreams — one was the dream the wise men from the East had after they had seen and worshiped the Christ child; the other was Joseph's. Joseph seems to have been directed and guided by dreams more than anything else in the crucial decisions he had to make about Mary and Jesus. In this, he was a bit like Radar O'Reilly in *M*A*S*H,* who had the ability to hear helicopters before anyone else could hear them; he had a kind of sixth sense, a special type of intuition. When Colonel Potter took over command of *M*A*S*H* 4077, one of the first things he asked of Radar, as they were decorating the walls of the office, was "Why (are you called) Radar?" The corporal/company clerk answered, "Sometimes I can tell what's gonna happen before it happens." Almost immediately, he lifted his head, tilted it back, and looked up toward the ceiling. "What is it?" Colonel Potter asked him.

"Choppers, sir," he answered. "I don't hear anything," said the colonel. In a moment, he heard what Radar had sensed many seconds before the noise was within the range of human hearing. That's why he was called Radar. Perhaps Joseph should have been called "Dreamer," or something akin to that, because he seems to have had a similar gift. And, since he took his dreams seriously, Jesus' life was saved when Joseph acted upon that dream and took Mary and Jesus to Egypt.

By this time, Joseph must have been on rather intimate terms with the angel, who came to him in his dreams. There's a significant difference between Radar's intuition and Joseph's dreams; God made the dreams happen and used them to get his messages to Joseph. There could be no mistaking the fact that the dream and the visit of the angel came from God the Father. God would not allow Jesus to be killed in the manner which Herod had prescribed for the boys under two years of age who were living in Bethlehem. Jesus had been born to die as a young man on a cross, not as an infant by a despot's sword; God's plan would not be thwarted by any Jewish king. So, God dispatched the angel in a dream sequence and Joseph got the meaning of the dream and did what God asked of him.

Another Joseph, hundreds of years after the first Joseph was sold into slavery by his jealous brothers, goes to Egypt. Isn't it odd that Egypt was both a refuge and a place of torment for the Israelites? The Jews and the Egyptians seem to be fighting much of the time, but when they aren't fighting, they appear to be the best of friends. The peace treaty signed by the Egyptians and the Israelites at Camp David a few years ago was a long time coming. But it was completely-logical, and maybe that's why President Jimmie Carter pushed it so hard. The two nations owe each other a lot, and they should be the best of friends. God has always had a hand in bringing them together. Through the angel in the dream, God gave Joseph a specific warning that Christ was in danger and, later, visited him again and told him it was time to return to Israel.

Surely, if Joseph and Mary didn't realize how special a child had been placed in their care, they knew it now. God himself protects Jesus and he needs only one angel, not a legion of them, to do it. He is not only loving and kind, but God is powerful, too. All life is sacred to him; every child is precious and, just as he wanted the baby Jesus to live, he wants all children protected. Our newspaper carried a story about the cancellation of a Boy Scout camp-out because a man had threatened the lives of some of the boys. The spokesman, who made the announcement, said: "We cancelled everything (several troops were to have programs at this particular camp). We don't want to be held ransom forever, but we felt we didn't have complete control in this case. We could have put out thousands of volunteers to help us patrol the area, but if one kid got hurt, it wouldn't be worth it." He explained that a man named John had written a letter threatening to kill three scouts and take three others captive; he had also called the home of one of the scouts and threatened to kill the boy if he went to the camp-out.[18] Instead of a newspaper and a phone call, God used a dream and an angel to warn Joseph that an attempt would be made upon Jesus' life; whatever plans he may have had to return to Nazareth were immediately scrapped and, as directed, Joseph bundled up Mary and the baby and left for Egypt.

The odd thing about this incident is God allowed Herod to go through with his terrible plan to kill all of the boys in Bethlehem who were under two years of age. And Herod did just that. There was weeping and wailing "in Ramah" — Bethlehem, in this case:

A voice was heard in Ramah,
wailing and loud lamentation,
Rachel weeping for her children;
she refused to be consoled,
because they were no more.

One wonders, at times, if God does hear the mourning for the innocent children who are slaughtered unmercifully in the wars of humanity. The complaint of the atheist, who says, "I can't believe in a God who allows little children to suffer and die," seems to be valid, sometimes. Why didn't God step in and stop Herod from murdering the baby boys of Bethlehem? Find the answer to that question and we will be able to comprehend why he doesn't intervene in all of those awful situations in which little children are made to suffer, to die, or are left to starve to death.

Today is not only the First Sunday after Christmas, when we are supposed to remember the flight to Egypt, but it is also Holy Innocents Day. We are asked to remember that slaughter in Bethlehem after Christ was born, no matter how much it intrudes on our lovely Christmas celebrations. As we give God thanks for the Christ child and for protecting him when his life might have been snuffed out, we need to remember we can and must do something to protect and help all of the children of the world. We must continually pray and work for peace throughout the world, so what we sing at Christmas time will become reality:

Glory to God in the highest,
and on earth peace among men
with whom he is pleased.

Israel, Egypt and all nations must become friends who honestly respect one another. God wants us to *promote peace* all over the world, not simply talk about it or yearn for it. Christians are peacemakers by nature and by God's design.

We Christians need to be engaged in activites which will alter the life-styles of people in refugee camps, who desperately need relief and assistance. Someone has said Americans react generously when a physical crisis occurs, such as the recent famine in Ethiopia (and other parts of Africa, as well as the rest of the world), but we soon forget the need and go on to something else. Perhaps one function of Holy Innocents Day is to keep us alert to the crises that remain with us. Lutheran Social Service of Minnesota recently reminded us we need to be alert: "CRISIS ALERT — DON'T ABANDON THE CHILDREN OF CAMBODIA'S KILLING FIELDS. Since 1978, the U.S. has resettled over 100,000 Cambodian refugees who had fled the horrors of the Bol Pot regime and, more recently, the Vietnamese occupation of their country. The Cambodian exodus has not stopped. Today, there are close to 40,000 refugees in Khao I Dang, a camp under the protection of the United Nations High Commissioner for Refugees. An additional 230,000 Cambodians are on or near the . . .border . . ." [19] Food, clothing, medicine, and resettlement efforts are needed in the light of this and other crises.

But Christians have to use their imaginations and ingenuity to work for more permanent solutions to the various problems that plague the people, especially the babies and children, of the world. Dr. Arthur Rouner, pastor of the Colonial Church of Edina, Minnesota, has become involved in one such project. He has raised five million dollars that will be spent to drill wells, build dams, and construct irrigation ditches in the Ansokia Valley of Ethiopia. He plans to take the money to Ethiopia and see that the project is properly begun. He said: "I'm excited because I think this is the most important thing I or our people could be doing in the world at this time. I don't see anything more important to be doing than trying to save those lives . . . I feel that I've been given a chance to be about the most significant enterprise that I could have (been involved in) . . . I'm scared (because)...there's a lot of risk involved in terms of what you can accomplish, but I believe it's worth the try." There's no question in my mind that's the sort of thing God wants done in this world, in order to save the little children, and you and I are the ones he wants to do it.

Where was God, the God who warned Joseph in a dream to get out of Bethlehem and take refuge in Egypt, when the baby boys were slain by Herod? One thing is sure and certain: he was weeping with the parents of those children, just as he does when innocent children die today. He couldn't step in and intervene then, any- more than he can right now, but he does expect us to act, on his behalf, to save the children of the world. Jesus was delivered by a dream. Children and babies today will have to be saved by courageous, imaginative, and forthright action by those who are able to help. He has given us a direct command, not a dream, to get busy and do what has to be done.

Jesus — the Holiest Name

(Note: This is the shortest text in the lectionary. It poses the problem of how to preach on it. Should the preacher simply construct what used to be known as a textual sermon, emphasizing and expounding a single verse of the Bible, or are there other homiletical possibilities? I suggest it has to be preached in the context of the Christmas story and as the heart of the Christmas cycle. A type of story sermon suggests itself, which picks up the story, but also allows the specific text to speak. Should the text be used at a watchnight service on December 31, a slightly different approach would have to be made: "Jesus — the Name that Makes All Things New.")

For most of the past decade, a local man has been attempting to change his name from Michael Herbert Dengler to 1069 (pronounced One Zero Six Nine by Mr. Dengler). He has taken his case to court, but has been turned down on the grounds that it is totally inappropriate; it has no meaning. Mr. Dengler argues it does have meaning, at least to him. The numbers reflect the cosmic nature of his life, he says, "The one expresses his oneness with the universe, while zero shows his relationship with 'time in movement through life.' The six represents his spatial occupancy in the universe, and nine stands for 'the relationship I have to essence in the difference in the meaning of actualizing the spatially ever-present nature of life'." His latest attempt to get his name changed to 1069 involves applying for a license to marry a young woman; he has indicated, on the marriage license, that 1069 is applying for the license as Michael Io Holtz. If he can get the certificate issued that way, he will argue that the city accepted the change from 1069 to Michael Io Holtz, and this constitutes legal recognition of 1069 as his name. Needless to say, the city attorney has been apprised of the situation and is taking steps to block this latest move of Mr. Dengler to acquire a four digit number as a new name.[20]

No one opposed the name Jesus for the baby boy born to Mary and his earthly father, Joseph. Nor were there any questions like the ones asked of Elizabeth at the circumcision and naming of John the Baptizer. Unlike Zechariah, Joseph was able to speak, and, undoubtedly, it was he who said, "His name is Jesus." Mary knew, of course, about Joseph's dream and was well aware the angel had given Joseph a name for the baby, as well as the truth about Mary's pregnancy. The angel's directive, which came from God, prevailed, as far as they were concerned; they knew for almost the entire term of her pregnancy what the baby would be named. They never knew the problem people have trying to decide upon a name for their first-born child. The angel had said, "...you shall call his name Jesus . . ." and they did, because that's the name God had given him before his birth.

The name of a child, to the Hebrews and to Christians as well, was supposed to have some connection to the will and purposes of God, especially as these had been expressed in the lives of parents, family, relatives, or other special people. Along with circumcision, it was a sign of participating in God's covenant with Israel. From the perspective of God's people, there really is something in a name. My parents learned this when they got to the font for my brother's baptism. He was Ted to them, and they wanted him to be baptized as Ted. But the pastor refused their request on the grounds that Ted was a nickname; he insisted that he had to be named Theodore — "gift of God" — and he was. He was sickly as an infant, and a family physician told my grandparents, "He won't live to be a year old." But he did. Theodore became his legal, as well as his baptismal, name. But he was always known as Ted and, years later, he went to court to change his name from Theodore, which never really suited him, to Ted. The court, at least, had no problems with Ted, as long as that is what he wanted to be called. I doubt that many pastors, today, would insist a literal biblical and Christian name would have to be used. The parents' wishes, without any consideration of Christian concerns, seem to be what determines how a child shall be named; this makes the process no less serious, because the name may have special meaning for them, as the name Jesus had for God and Mary and Joseph, too.

Jesus' name has eternal significance for all people in that it sharply defines his mission to "save his people from their sins." It means more than simply saying, "God is with you," because it means "God was in Christ, reconciling the world to himself." His name was a constant reminder to Jesus, for Mary and Joseph had told him those fantastic stories about his birth, that God would be with him in all he did to complete the mission his Father had decreed for him. In the introduction to his, *The Stories of Ray Bradbury,* Bradbury calls himself "that special freak, the man with the child inside who remembers all. I remember the day and the hour I was born. I remember being circumcised on the second day after my birth. I remember sucking at my mother's breast. Years later I asked my mother about the circumcision. I had information that couldn't have been told me; there was no reason to tell a child, especially in those still-Victorian times. Was I circumcised somewhere away from the lying-in hospital? I was. My father took me to the doctor's office. I remember the doctor. I remember the scalpel."[21] There was reason to tell Jesus about his circumcision and why he was named Jesus. The Gospels do not say that Jesus remembered his birth and the incidents connected to it. His parents must have told him those lovely stories and as they much as they knew of their meaning. God would be with him in all he did. Indeed, he would need the comfort of his Father's presence and Spirit in the lonely business that lay ahead of him. He didn't realize, when he was told those tales about his birth, that he would be surrounded by enemies who hated him enough to kill him, but he soon learned how much he needed the Father's love and assurance when he began his ministry. At times, it must have seemed the whole world was against him, that he was entirely on his own.

One day, I went out on our back porch and frightened a pair of little Black-capped Chickadees in the lower branches of a spruce tree close to the door. They flew off in protest and then I discovered why they had been there; a nestling was on the lowest branch of the tree, apparently on its first outing from the nest. I know it could not fly, or hadn't really tried to; it didn't move from the branch, despite the fact that it was facing me. I quickly got out of sight and waited for the parents to return to their young one, but they didn't come back while I watched. A couple hours later I returned and the young bird was still on that lower branch; the parent birds were nowhere in sight. Had I scared them away permanently? Had they been so frightened that they would abandon their baby? Would that little bird have to spend the night there with no one to watch over it?

I wondered if it could survive on its own. Just before dark, I sneaked around the house to a vantage point and, to my relief, the parent birds were there, feeding their young one; they had not abandoned the baby bird and they wouldn't leave it to its own devices until it learned to fly and care for itself. God would go even farther with Jesus; he would be with him always, "even unto death," and Jesus would need all the loving support he could get before his ministry was completed.

Jesus' name was destined to become a loved and revered name to those who believed him to be the Son of God and the Savior of the world. William Walsham How's hymn to the Name of Jesus did not make it from the *Service Book and Hymnal* of the American Lutheran Church and the Lutheran Church in America into the *Lutheran Book of Worship* of the same two Lutheran bodies. It had a common life of about twenty years and, for some reason, was eliminated. But it seems to sum up what the Name of Jesus really means and why it is so dearly loved by most Christians:

Jesus, Name of wondrous love,
Name all other names above!
Unto which must every knee
Bow in deep humility.

Jesus, Name of priceless worth
To the fallen sons of earth,
For the promise that it gave,
"Jesus shall his people save."

Jesus, only Name that's given
Under all the mighty heaven,
Whereby man, to sin enslaved,
Bursts his fetters and is saved.[22]

Paul put it right when he said "at the name of Jesus every knee shall bow . . . and every tongue confess that Jesus Christ is Lord to the glory of God the Father."

But every knee has not bowed, never has, in fact, for Jesus' name, and Jesus was hated by his enemies. He learned what it means to be despised and detested by people he had come to help and to save. The last three years of his life must have been a terrible shock to him; to be despised by people, to the point of hatred, must have been almost too much to take. Jesus' experience must have been something like that of Neil Simon, only worse. Simon's award-winning play, *Biloxi Blues,* is about a lot of things, but especially about anti-Semitism; he was writing about his own experiences as a Jew. After his parents were divorced, Simon went to Woodside High School in New York City: "I sat down in school, never aware that it would mean anything that I was Jewish. They asked me my name. I said, 'Simon,' and the entire class burst out laughing. It had never occurred to me that anyone would laugh at the name Simon. The kid in front of me turned around and said, 'Where'd you get that name?' Someone else said, 'That's a Jewish name, isn't it?' And slowly it dawned on me — I was 13 and had never lived in a neighborhood without a significant number of Jews — that I was different. That I was the only Jew in the school." Simon went out for baseball and became the best hitter on the team and, after that, he says, "nobody bothered me any more." But there was another boy whom they'd call 'Kike' and things like that, as they had Neil Simon; he couldn't play baseball and the insults continued. *"Biloxi Blues"* was written partly on his behalf. At the time those things were happening, Simon did nothing because he didn't know what to do. He does now.[23]

And Jesus? He simply let them put him to death, crucify him on Golgotha and in that strange way, God's mysterious wisdom, he saved his people from their sins. They did succeed in taking away his name, Jesus, in the hour of his suffering and death, but Pilate had another sign prepared and nailed above his head, "The King of the Jews." So Jesus became the Christ, the Savior of all people.

Reflection Time

Here we are on the eleventh day of Christmas, with Epiphany and the Star, the Wise Men, and the baby Jesus a couple of days ahead of us, and, all of a sudden, we are whisked back to Advent and, behind it, to the very beginning of creation. "In the beginning was the Word, and the Word was with God, and the Word was God." That's all there was when God went into action, created our solar system, the earth and everything on it, including the human race "in his image." Few of us are ready for such a head-trip; more than likely, we are still thinking about the new year, the various football "bowl" games, rather than Christmas, Epiphany, or Advent. But today, Advent calls us to review what has happened in the light of Christmas and Epiphany, whether or not we are at all ready for this.

Toward the end of the season that celebrates the birth of Jesus, we are confronted by two, not one, grown men, John the Baptizer and Jesus. It seems the Evangelist, John, who wrote this book, wanted to set the record straight, or at least clarify the relationship of John the Baptizer and Jesus. John's is a supporting role to the character in the drama, Jesus the Messiah; his ministry was different, his way of life was radically divergent to that of Jesus, and his preaching became totally dissimilar to Jesus' preaching. John, after baptizing Jesus, might have found himself at odds with the Lord and, instead of supporting him, could have denounced the One who came as Messiah. Matthew's question comes to us again: "Are you the One who is to come or should we look for another?" It is strange how people engaged in the same religious endeavor may differ so emphatically that they become enemies and do more harm than good to the cause.

In the summer of 1985, over 40,000 Southern Baptists gathered in Dallas for the convention of their church. It was the largest convention that the Southern Baptists ever had, and with good reason; a theological dispute over the interpretation of the Bible had arisen between various factions of the denomination and threatened to cause a split among the conservatives and the moderates. Dr. Charles Stanley was the spokesman for the conservatives, who hold a fundamental conception of the literal truth of the Holy Bible, while the moderates were led by Dr. Winfred Moore, who has been influenced by the so-called liberal biblical scholarship. The two sides of the controversy are in essential agreement on most other theological matters, but this disagreement could cause the denomination to be split into two groups over a matter which cannot be settled in a convention. Something like that could have happened to John the Baptizer and Jesus, but it didn't, and the Evangelist wants us to know that. Perhaps he wants his readers, then and now, to be united in their understanding of the fundamental truths about Jesus and his God-given mission.

Today, we look at Jesus' story from the perspective of an evangelist who is able to discern God's gracious love and mercy inserted into the world in the life and ministry of Jesus. God's intention, from the very beginning, was to forgive and preserve rather than condemn his children for their deliberate sins and wickedness. Why did he exempt Noah and his family, instead of wiping out the entire human-race and starting over again with some other kind of creatures? That would have been easier and far less painful than the action he initiated — sending his only Son into the world to die on a cross like a common criminal. Couldn't God create, after this one failure, a more perfect race "in his image," beings who would choose God and good instead of Satan and sin? It might have been worth a try. But that was not in God's character; he knew that what he had done at the beginning was good and he planned to set things right between his people and himself through Jesus. Surely, God was "in Christ reconciling the world to himself."

Jesus must have wondered about the meaning of all the stories told him from the time he was a little child until he was baptized by John. They were important to him, just as they are important to our understanding and the development of our faith. Those tales helped him to perceive his relationship with the Father and to comprehend the role John was to have in his mission in the world. Can't you picture the child Jesus asking his mother, "Tell me the story about John," or "Sing the song the angels sang the night I was born"? These stories clarified for him the reason he had been born and what he was to do in the world. Russell Baker, in his *Growing Up,* tells about a Christmas at his grandparents' house when he was very young: " 'Merry Christmas'!" my grandmother said, taking me from my father and thrusting my nose against the pine needles (of the Christmas tree). 'Kris Kringle's been here. Look what he brought for you.' It was a toy steam shovel with metal teeth and a 'string mechanism,' (so that) the shovel could be lifted into the air and its bottom released to dump . . . dirt back onto the ground." Baker writes: "To my grandmother and father and uncles it must have seemed like an educational toy. Metalworkers, stonemasons, carpenters, people with a tradition of craftsmanship and building, they naturally assumed that giving me a toy steam shovel was giving me something more lasting than a toy. They were also giving me a way to start thinking about my life. Left to her own devices, my mother, I suspect, would not have thought of such a beautiful, ingenious machine but would have given me a book."[24] Mary, without a doubt, told Jesus the stories about John's birth and his own birth in Bethlehem, how they had to go to Egypt, and why they settled in Nazareth. They were vitally important to the way he thought about his life.

God's intention became reality, not simply in the birth of Jesus, but in the quality of his life, as well. Truly, he did "dwell among us" and, truly, he was "full of grace and truth." He was a whole human being, and, therefore, holy in the eyes of faithful people and God; there was nothing false or phony about Jesus Christ, of that we may be sure! What a contrast we discover between Christ and ourselves from this perspective. A few years ago, Ellen Goodman wrote a column for the new year, "Forswearing the credit card habit." For the past several years, she writes, she has been observing a kind of financial Lent: "I give up plastic (credit cards)." But she has been disappointed in herself and has determined that it has been a "phony" exercise: "To be frank, my plan was born out of a desire to strengthen my moral fibre as much as my financial picture." It hasn't worked, she concludes: "This is not a phony poverty vow: Let's all pretend we're poor and eat on a welfare budget this week for the bourgois fun of it. It is rather a phony moral vow: Let's all pretend that we are beyond the reach of crass material values and abandon consumerism for a month just for the virtue of it."[25]

She realizes such acts may deceive others, but we cannot delude ourselves into thinking we are really good people, of infinite value to people and God, by making such vows and even keeping them. There is One, only one person, Jesus, who is true and holy in the eyes of God, and you and I are meant to realize this fact and recognize Jesus for who and what he is. Jesus, the One sent by God, did live among us as the only person completely "full of grace and truth."

"We have beheld his glory" — these last few days, in particular — in the "Word become flesh and dwelt among us" as "the only Son from the Father." God's glory surrounded the Christ in all of the events when he was born, and for that we are humble and thankful people. Because we know the rest of the story, we see the fulness of that glory in his death and resurrection, together with the impact of his life and death upon people in this world. His glory is reflected in our expressions of faith and our attempts to serve him and his people in this world. It is fitting, in the light of Christmas and the rest of his story, that a nine-year-old child should develop a game aimed at stopping war. Michelle Alexander, it was recently reported, has developed a board game that she calls "Give Peace a Chance" as a project in her class for gifted children in Fresno, California. It is a game of the superpowers, the United States and the Soviet Union, and is won by the country (player) who "declares itself a nuclear-free zone." While the game is tilted toward compromise by these powers, it contains positive suggestions for attaining peace, such as (on landing on one space), "Welcome to Geneva, shake hands and smile." Players (countries) gain points "when they share an invention that benefits both countries or when they extend an invitation to children from the opponent's country (to visit their's)." Players also lose points for "invading a smaller country . . . or for rejecting a compromise in arms negotiations." In a paper explaining the game, Michelle wrote, "I invented this game to stop war. The object is to get the most points, hopefully by compromising and making your country a nuclear-free zone. This means the children of the world will be able to grow up."[26] Well-intentioned, but a bit naive and childlike? What do you have to say about saving the world by dying on a cross in the middle of a garbage dump? There's not much glory, or hope, in that. Was Jesus a bit deluded when he declared, "And I, if I be lifted up will draw all people to myself"? We look to his resurrection and ascension and then, indeed, we see the fulness of his glory.

Christmas is about to end for another year and, before long, it will be Lent, when Jesus' glory gets tarnished a bit. But Easter will come, then, perhaps, we may dare to remember the story of how he came into the world as a helpless child, how he grew to manhood, preached, taught, and healed for three years before his passion and death, because we remember, and can sing again, the angels' song, "Glory to God in the highest, and peace to people on earth with whom he is pleased." In his incarnation we find the grace and truth of God, and he has set us free.

Matthew 2:1-12 *The Epiphany of our Lord (January 6)*

A Star - and Yet Another Dream

Picture two men, out in the fields among a flock of sheep, looking up toward the night sky. One says, "It isn't there any more." The other, Loren Eiseley, comments: "He was the only man I ever knew who hunted for bones in the stars, and I remember we were standing out among his sheep in the clear starshine when he said it. 'It isn't there any more,' he repeated. And innocently enough I asked, 'What isn't?' — not really thinking at all but just making conversation and watching the silver light drifting over the gray backs of the sheep. 'The fifth planet,' he answered."

Eiseley was an anthropologist, not even an amateur astronomer, as was his friend, but he knew something about the solar system. He writes: "I thought a minute and counted in my head twice to make sure, and then I said a little soothingly, as one talks to a confused child, 'But the fifth planet is Jupiter. There it is over there. All you have to do is swing the tripod around and you'll pick it up all right. Planets don't disappear that easy, thank God.' But his friend answered, 'The fifth one did all the same'." He believed there was a planet between Mars and Jupiter which exploded, and if he looked hard and long enough, he would discover its remains in the heavens and learn why it blew up. He was looking for a star that had disappeared. It was almost like "Twinkle, twinkle, little star. How I wonder where you are."[27]

Some time after the shepherds were visited in the fields outside of Bethlehem, one or more astronomers who lived "in the East" finally saw what they had been looking for in the skies. A special star appeared one night and, immediately, a group of them began a journey to Jerusalem because they believed that the star heralded the birth of a very special king. The story of the star is real enough; even some modern astronomers believe that part of the story. Professor Karlis Kaufmanis, an astronomer at the University of Minnesota, is confident such a star appeared about the time Jesus was born. His popular lecture, "The Star of Bethlehem," which he has delivered to church groups thousands of times, explains his theory of how the star appeared in the sky and could be seen in the part of the world where Jesus was born. He is convinced that the confluence of two planets, which came close enough to shine as one bright star, is the explanation for the star's existence. It is a phenomenon that occurs regularly every so many centuries. The star was real and the wise men, or their astronomers, saw it and believed it to be a sign of the birth of the "king of the Jews." So they followed it. How they knew the meaning of the star will forever remain a mystery. Perhaps they were mystics and one of them, as happens toward the end of this story, had a dream in which an angel spoke to him and told him to follow the star to its destination — the birthplace of this new-born king. They did follow the star, at any rate, and ultimately reached Jerusalem and asked the first people they met, "Where is he who has been born king of the Jews? For we have seen his star in the East, and have come to worship him."

"What are you talking about?" may have been the reply, because no one in Jerusalem had heard anything about Herod's wife having a new son; and he wouldn't be heir to the throne anyway, for Herod had another son, Archelaus, who was to succeed him as King of Israel. What they had to say must have seemed nonsense to those who heard about them, except for one man, Herod, who was informed about the visitors and their questions and took seriously what he had been told. So Herod invited the wise men to the palace for a conference and, after he had consulted the chief priesfs, informed them this king was to be born in Bethlehem. He gave them orders to return to him, after they had found the child, and tell him exactly where the child was so he might go and worship him, too. Herod was shook up by what he had heard. They told him a tall tale, but he was insecure enough about his throne so that he believed it. Right then and there, the first of many plots to kill Jesus took shape. Herod and the religious leaders would not be satisfied until Jesus was put to death.

It didn't matter to Herod that God had something to do with the birth of Jesus. He was not concerned in the least that the long-awaited Messiah, who was to "set his people free," had finally been born. He didn't care a bit that this one might lead a mighty revolt and throw off the yoke of the hated Roman Empire forever. All Herod was concerned with was protecting his throne; he wanted to be king as long as he could, even if the circumstances of his kingship were less than ideal and, in the eyes of the Roman authorities, he was only a puppet-king. That was better than not being king at all, or being hauled off to Rome to be tried and executed, or worse,should he be suspected of complicity in some sort of a plot against the Roman Emperor. If this were any sort of Divine Plan, he wouldn't have any part of it; he wanted to keep God out of the picture, and that's why he set out to thwart the prophesies by killing the infant boys in Bethlehem.

Herod is no different than many of us where the will of God is concerned. We know it. We believe it. But we resist God's will and any plan he may have for us and the world in which we live. When Loren Eiseley left his star-gazing friend, who was a rancher named Jim Radnor, he wrote, "I never expected to see him again." But he did visit him again, taking along some clippings on astronomical matters from the science section of the *New York Times*. His friend hardly glanced at them; he had burned all of his files. Eiseley said: "It's a clear night and I reckon you can show me a lot now," starting to move toward the door. "I don't look anymore," Radnor said. "I don't look anymore because I know . . . I know about it already . . . I believed in the plan, . . . what some people call the Divine Plan. I believed in life. I believed it was advancing, rising, becoming more intelligent. I believed it might have been farther along out there . . . I believed it would give us hope to know . . . The Plan is not what you think . . . and life . . ." Five years later Eiseley received a card from Radnor; it came one week after Hiroshima. There was one line on the card: "The Plan is not what you think it is. Do you see now?" Eiseley writes: "For a time I puzzled over it, unsure that I did. But after Nagasaki the thing began to be a tune in my head like the little songs the wind makes under telegraph wires. It just went on sighing. 'You see? You see?' Of course I knew he was crazy, but just the same he was right about one thing. The fifth planet is gone. And maybe I see."[28] The star is gone, but Christ lives. Do we see with the eyes of faith? Or do we believe God has been thwarted by the resistance and sin of human beings, so we have no hope?

The wise men from the East followed the star to Bethlehem, found the child, made their visit, and did obeisance to Jesus, and returned to their country by another route. One or more of them had dreamed they should not return to Herod in Jerusalem, but should go home without stopping to see him. Regardless of that, they became the first Christian pilgrims; they made a long and arduous journey to the Holy Land as pilgrims. They went there to worship "the king of the Jews" and they did just that, giving him precious gifts in the process. They worshiped One whom they believed was sent by God, while Herod, who is typical of human beings, really worshiped no one but himself.

There's a fascinating science-fiction story, "Trojan Horse," by Michael Swanwick, which, as part of the plot, tells about a Star Maker project using (computer) "wetware" to program the brains of people who have to live in space. One of the characters, Donna Landis, S.J, (the author imagines that the Roman Catholic Church is not only ordaining women but that they, in this advanced time, are able to join the select order of the Society of Jesus) explains the project: "The Star Maker is a piece of experimental theology that IGF dreamed up . . . it's basic research into the nature of the mind. The Vatican Synod (the author anticipates world-wide reunion of the Holy Catholic Church, too) is providing funding so we can keep an eye on it . . . This set of wetware will supposedly reshape a human mind into God. They want to computer-model the infinite. Anyway, the specs were drawn up, and it was tried out on — what was the name of the test subject?" "It doesn't matter." But it worked; they programmed a woman into believing that she was God, but they couldn't deprogram her. Landis explains: "What we didn't take into account, though, was that she'd *LIKE* being God. When we tried deprogramming her, she simply overrode our instructions and reprogrammed herself back up." Landis' companion remarked, "The poor woman . . . AND YET — WHAT A GLORIOUS EXPERIENCE TO BE GOD! Something within her thrilled to it. IT WOULD BE ALMOST WORTH THE PRICE."[29] People who worship themselves rather than God, as Herod did, are not unfamiliar with that feeling of exhilaration. But, at the end of the Christmas season, we are reminded again that we are called to be pilgrim people, who join the wise men in their worship of Jesus, not simply as the king of the Jews but as the King of Kings and Lord of Lords.

The wise men went back to "the East" and were never heard of again, except in unsubstantiated legends. Once more, we, too, are reinserted into the world with a prayer of thanksgiving on our lips. As much as we would like to, we can't stay and worship, basking in the glory of his birth. For we live by the Word of God, not by a dream, and his work needs to be done in the world.

Matthew 3:13-17 *The Baptism of our Lord (Epiphany 1)*

Death by Water

Thirty years have passed in the last five days on the church calendar. Jesus was still a baby just days ago, when Matthew's version of the Christmas story was read and Christ's Epiphany was celebrated around the world. Now Jesus is at the beginning of his ministry, and we remember his baptism by John the Baptizer in the Jordan River; he has but three more years to preach, teach, and heal and then he will die on a criminal's cross, despite the fact that he did no wrong. We know, at the very beginning of his ministry the end of it was almost in sight. His baptism was the beginning of his death; he died by water before he died on Calvary.

John the Baptizer was attracting great crowds of people with his preaching, "Repent and be baptized for the kingdom of heaven is at hand," when Jesus was about thirty years of age. He was also very successful in making enemies of the religious leaders of the Jews, because he called them things like "brood of snakes" and threatened them with his predictions which, in effect, said "One who comes after me will clean out the corrupt leaders of the Temple" and "throw the chaff into the fire." John was no diplomat; he called a spade a spade and, in his eyes, the religion of the Hebrews had been corrupted by various chief priests and Pharisees. That corruption had to be wiped out. He believed that the Coming One, the Messiah, would do just that. Popular among many people who knew he was right and sought baptism by him for the forgiveness of their sins, John was equally despised by the religious and the royalty in Jerusalem. His enemies won the day, you will recall, and brought his ministry to a premature conclusion, but not before he accomplished what God wanted him to do. In John's case, it was royalty, not religion, which did the dirty work.

One day, Jesus appeared with the crowds of people being baptized by John at the river. John recognized him (perhaps he had been expecting him to be attracted by his ministry), but he wasn't prepared for Jesus to seek baptism at his hands. Surprised, he said to Jesus, "I need to be baptized by you." John knew his role in God's drama of forgiveness and reconciliation that would unfold in the ministry of Jesus; Christ was to predominate, while John's was a supporting role. Jesus was the Messiah, and not John, no matter how large a following he had built up into what could be called the beginning of a "baptist" sect, and he, according to Scripture, was the "forerunner" of Jesus, sent "to prepare his way and make the paths straight." It was not for him to baptize Jesus; it should have been the other way around and John knew it.

John saw Jesus as the sinless One, ordained by God to save his people from their sins; it would take a sinless person to do that. And that was a major difference between Jesus and John, and between Jesus and us. "All have sinned and fallen short of the glory of God" is not a slogan nor a simplistic maxim; it is a fact, with one exception — Jesus of Nazareth. In his writing, *Against the Pelagians,* St. Jerome includes an interesting little story from *The Gospel According to the Hebrews:* "The mother of Jesus and his brothers said to him, 'John the Baptist baptizes for the forgiveness of sins; let us go and be baptized by him.' But he said to them, 'In what have I sinned that I should go and be baptized by him? Unless, perhaps, what I have just said is a sin of ignorance'."[30] That may or may not have the ring of an authentic saying of Jesus, but it does express what John knew — that Jesus was without sin and, in that way, differed from all the people being baptized — and from us.

The need for forgiveness is one thing we have in common with John the Baptizer; his "I need to be baptized by you" implied part of the message that he had been preaching, "for the forgiveness of sins." It is through baptism that God gives us the greatest gift he can offer us — forgiveness, the assurance we will share eternity with him through the mercy of Jesus. Any sin, every sin, may be forgiven by God when we repent and are baptized "in the name of the Father, and of the Son, and of the Holy Spirit." The television mini-series of *The Martian Chronicles,* omitted one significant incident included in the book. Sam Parkhill, who had been on one of the early missions to Mars, returned to Mars with his wife to build a fast-food stand; he anticipated the mass colonization of Mars by people from Earth and he was going to be ready to make his fortune. After the hot dog stand is completed, one of the Old Ones — a Martian, who had given him approval to construct the stand — appears and says, "Mr. Parkhill, I've come back to speak to you again." Parkhill answers, "Go and hide in the hills, that's where you belong." "We mean you no harm," answers the Martian. "But I mean you harm," Sam replies, and when the Martian reaches for a bronze tube, Sam draws his gun, fires, and the Martian disintegrates before their eyes. The tube turns out to be just that, not a weapon at all, and it contains a document written in Martian script. Sam cannot make it out; it's a mystery to him.

Suddenly, a girl, who also gets shot, and other Martians appear, and then a chase scene begins, with Sam and his wife in one of the ancient Martian sand-ships being pursued by Martians, who, after he has killed several more, finally corner Sam and his wife. Sam cries for mercy: "I didn't do anything . . . It was all a mistake . . . And that Martian . . . his death was an accident." Sam throws down his gun, "I give up . . . don't kill me." They don't. The leader pulls out another bronze tube, interprets the document it contains for Sam and his wife — it is a deed to 100,000 square miles of Mars; and then he gives him six more deeds like the first one. Sam, who deserves to die for his murderous deeds to the Martians, is forgiven and given title to half of Mars by the Old Ones, who send him back to his hot dog stand.[31] That's the way God works. He forgives us and gives us a place in heaven itself, when all we deserve is condemnation and death. And the means of conveying his loving grace and mercy to us is through the Sacrament of Holy Baptism and the Eucharist, which renews the gift of forgiveness and reconciliation we received in baptism. Like John, we need to be baptized by Jesus "in the name of the Father, and the Son, and the Holy Spirit" for the forgiveness of sins, reunion with the Father, and the promise of eternal life.

Jesus didn't need baptism for the forgiveness of sins, but he needed baptism. He needed to be baptized by John to affirm the role of servant in his public life and ministry. As servant, he would establish a new covenant between God and his people:

I have given you as a covenant to the people,
a light to the nations,
to open the eyes that are blind,

to bring out the prisoners from the dungeon,
from the prison those who sit in darkness.

The leaders of the Jews, and probably many of the people, didn't think they needed that kind of Messiah, a Suffering Servant, but that's what God offered them in Jesus. And that's the kind of Christ we need if we are honest with ourselves and really face up to our deepest needs of forgiveness and assurance and the comfort of knowing he is with us in this life when we need him.

A few weeks ago, my wife called one of our neighbors to make arrangements to pick up our granddaughter and their daughter after basketball practice. The young mother suddenly broke down and said, "I've got cancer. I just came from the clinic, where they did a biopsy on my breast. I have to have a mastectomy on Friday of this week." She was beside herself with fear and trepidation and, at this point, could not be comforted. But, as the time for her operation drew near, the people in the neighborhood rallied around her. There are sixteen homes on our little side street, and when my wife contacted each of the neighbors to have them sign a get-well card and to collect money for flowers, a community of concerned people emerged in a typical suburban setting where normally there is not much evident concern. A man who seems rather remote from his neighbors, said, "I'll pray for her." A Roman Catholic woman wrote on the card, "I'll pray for you, Kathy." Nearly everyone on the street made some comment, or wrote something of that sort on the card. For a time, there was a bit of a community in Christ existing in the midst of a life-threatening crisis. People seemed to believe it would do some good to pray to God for the woman with cancer, and Jesus would hear and answer their prayers on her behalf and be with her as she faced an uncertain future. That's one of the gifts of baptism which we have because Jesus became the Suffering Servant who joined us in baptism?

When Jesus came up out of the water, John knew that he was right when he had said, "I need to be baptized by you," because the Spirit of God descended like a dove and a voice announced, "This is my beloved Son, with whom I am well pleased." Both Jesus and John knew they had done the correct thing, and Jesus' baptism was fully accepted by his Father in heaven. This suggests that every baptism is an occasion for rejoicing in heaven, and God responds with the same blessed assurance to every person who is baptized. On those

Sundays when a child is baptized in the congregation to which we belong, a special banner is placed by the font. It announces to the congregation: "This is my beloved," and, under it, a smaller banner with "son" or "daughter" and the child's name upon it has been inserted in slots for this baptism, followed by "in whom I am well pleased." Through water and the Word and the Holy Spirit, we join him before the throne of God in the knowledge that our baptisms are pleasing to God and he accepts us, forever.

Thirty years have passed since we last listened to and reflected upon the story of Jesus' birth in our Sunday and Epiphany worship, but nearly two thousand years have passed since his baptism. The story of his baptism closes any time-gap for us and validates our baptisms, and gives us comfort and hope.[32]

John 1:29-34 (C, L)
John 1:29-41 (RC)

Epiphany 2 (C, L)
Ordinary Time 2 (RC)

The Lamb of God

I live next door to what could almost be called an international house. It was owned by a university mathematics professor when my wife and I bought our home. When he went to Europe on sabbatical leave, he rented the home to a visiting professor of mathematics from France. Later, he rented to a German family for a year, and a Danish family will be living in it for awhile, although a different family — presently in Switzerland on a two year business assignment — currently owns it. The Danish family was invited to a wedding in a local Lutheran Church; their daughter was a bridesmaid for another Danish girl who was being married. A week or so later, her mother brought over pictures of the wedding, the wedding party, her daughter, and some of the people at the reception. "It was a lovely wedding," she said, "but I was a little put off by a couple of things that happened. Your customs are different from ours," she told us. "What put you off?" my wife asked her. "The pastor announced, 'I am pleased to present to you, Mr. and Mrs . . .' That was the first thing that seemed odd to me; it seemed to take away some of the solemnity of the wedding. Our services are more formal." "What was the second thing?" we asked her. "This was even worse; the congregation applauded when the announcement was made. That seemed very strange to me. We never applaud anything in our churches."

Now it is the turn of the writer of the fourth Gospel, John, to tell his version of the baptism of Jesus at the hands of that other John, the Baptizer. It was the day after Jesus' baptism took place (John does not tell the actual story about the baptism). When

John saw Jesus, he made an announcement: "Behold, the Lamb of God, who takes away the sin of the world! This is he whom I said, 'After me comes a man who ranks before me, for he was before me . . .' " The Evangelist wanted the world to know two things: 1. The Messiah had come to accomplish God's intention of removing sin from the world; and, 2. There was no conflict between John and Jesus about which of them was to be the Messiah and deliver his people from their sins. There is no report about who comprised his audience, although it must have been to the crowds who came to hear him preach and to see him baptizing people in the Jordan that he spoke. Nor is there any evidence that anyone applauded when he made the announcement to the people. This must have been part of a sermon, and no one dared to applaud, even when the announcement was of such immediate and lasting importance to the hearers and to all people.

Think of the power struggle that might have occurred if John had believed that he was the One promised by God, the Messiah. Suppose he had said, "Jesus, whom I baptized, will be a great teacher and healer, but I am the Messiah, and I will deliver you from your sins." A state of utter confusion would exist, to say the least, and the beginning of Jesus' ministry would have been thrown into turmoil. Do you remember the tactics of Mehmet Ali Agca, the Turk who attempted to assassinate the Pope a few years ago, in his 1985 trial? He seemed to be attempting to create confusion by claiming he was Jesus Christ, and, therefore, he was doing the bidding of God in his attempt to rid the world of one who really wasn't on the side of God. From one twisted perspective, this could have been seen, if it were a genuine belief on his part, as a real power struggle.

Suppose Ali Agca had killed the pope when he shot him. What would have happened? Would he have claimed the right to the primary seat of authority in the Roman Catholic Church? At times, he seemed to be convinced that he was Jesus Christ, like when he responded to a question about the fate of Emanuela Orlandi, who was kidnapped in 1983, concerning a crime some have connected to the attempt on the pope's life: "It is certain that Orlandi is alive. She was certainly kidnapped by the powerful Masonic organization P2 of Licio Gelli (the Italian industrialist, and leader of the Masonic Lodge in Italy, who was imprisoned in a Swiss jail and escaped in 1983), because this organization knew with certainty that I am Jesus Christ."[33] We can dismiss his claim as an outright lie or simply as the words of a madman, but no one ever accused John the Baptizer of being mad. People would have listened if he had claimed the title of Messiah, and would have followed his teachings. Confusion, at best, would have resulted. If John had been mentally ill or otherwise convinced he was the Messiah, he might even have made the sort of attempt on Jesus' life that Agca made on the pope. And he might have succeeded, much as did Bryan Stanley, who lived in a small town in Wisconsin, believed himself to be Elijah, and ac tually killed Father John Rossiter, Ferdinand L. Roth, Sr , and William G. Hammes, because he was convinced that current liturgical changes, including liturgical leadership and the reading of the Bible by women, were wrong.[34] John did no such thing, made no such claims or charges against Jesus.

John wanted people to know the truth about Jesus; he refused to be caught up in any power struggle, because he knew it would have been of Satan, not of God. John the Evangelist's story about the baptism differs from the others because he contends that John the Baptist didn't know Jesus until after he had been baptized: "I myself did not know him." That seems a little odd. After all, they were cousins who lived less than a hundred miles apart, and both of them had been to Jerusalem for Passover and, possibly, other feasts. Surely, their families must have gotten together for such celebrations. He must have known Jesus, or at least knew what he looked like. Could it have been that the stories he heard from his parents about his birth and role in the coming of the Messiah had not made it clear Jesus was to be the Messiah? The import of those stories had to be a bit on the mind-boggling side.When the Holy Spirit descended on Jesus in the form of a dove, of which God had informed him (in a dream, and by an angel-?), he immediately said, "Behold the Lamb of God, who takes away the sin of the world!" No one is reported to have cheered or applauded that announcement. Few people applaud or cheer on hearing the good news.

In a way, that is appropriate, because the good news to us is bad news for Jesus. John didn't know it, but he was pronouncing a death sentence on Jesus when he declared, "Behold, the Lamb of God, who takes away the sin of the world!" Jesus would be sentenced to death, not for what he was and the ultimate good he had come to accomplish, but simply because his preaching tended to be against the best interests of the religious establishment. This is an area where religion and politics often join together in an insidious partnership.

In the case of Pope John Paul, at one time, Ali Agca insisted he had attempted to kill the pope on Soviet orders, because Lech Walesa and Solidarity represented a threat to the Polish government and to the best interests of the Soviet Union, and Pope John Paul was throwing his support behind Walesa and the union. More recently, leaders of the United Democratic Front coalition in South Africa announced that a plot exists to eliminate Bishop Desmond Tutu and other leaders supporting the efforts to end apartheid. The Rev. Frank Chicane said: "We have positive information that within hours we are to be eliminated." It is just possible that, sooner or later, someone will try to kill Bishop Tutu,[35] just as they killed Jesus. It took three years to do it, but Jesus was finally executed by the combined efforts of the religious and political leaders in Israel. They didn't know they were playing into the hands of God when they did it, any more than John knew he was pronouncing a death sentence on Jesus when he called him "The Lamb of God, who takes away the sin of the world."

That's what he was — the Lamb of God — and there can hardly be a better description of Jesus. He became the sacrifice for sin, offered to God so forgiveness and reconciliation could take place. It nearly always takes an actual death to wipe out heinous sin and the crimes against God and humanity associated with it. Two brief articles were stacked upon each other in the newspapers. The first one followed this headline: "Claims of Mengele death don't end search." Despite the report that Joseph Mengele's body had been found and exhumed from a grave in Brazil, the "Nazi hunters" were not convinced by the evidence. They would continue their search for the "Angel of Death" of Nazi concentration camp infamy until they had absolute proof that the corpse was Mengele's. The second article's headline read: "Behind the scenes/Bavarian town tries to shake stigma of the "Angel of Death." The town of Mengele-Gunzberg was named after his grandfather, whose farm-machinery factory put the town of Gunzberg on the map. The mayor said: "The people of this city are frustrated because their city (of 19,000 people) is forever identified with the personality of Mengele." People are forever saying, "Leave us in peace." One man said, "Everyone knows he was inhumane, but after 40 years, why make such a drama-out of it?" And another adds, articulating his frustration, "Maybe he did some bad things, some things which were bad for Germany, but what the Americans did at Dresden (more people, it is claimed, were killed in that WWII bombing than in either Hiroshima or Nagasaki) also wasn't so great."[36] Only death will wipe out those sins, just as it took the death of Christ to obliterate "the sin of the world" in the eyes of God. He was, most positively, "the Lamb of God," and he did, most certainly, "take the sin of the world" upon himself in terrible death on Calvary's cross.

When John made that startling announcement, "Behold, the Lamb of God, who takes away the sin of the world!" the day after Jesus was baptized, he confirmed what was said when the dove descended on Jesus, "This is my beloved Son, in whom I am well pleased." No one, as far as we know, even politely applauded or cheered. But applause and cheering might be in order now, because we know he was really the "Lamb of God" and he did take away the sin of the world — even ours. Glory Hallelujah!

Matthew 4:12-23 *Epiphany 3 (C, L)*
Ordinary Time 3 (RC)

Beginning a Ministry

Matthew and John, the two evangelists, seem to be at odds about the beginning of Jesus' ministry; they tell a rather different story. John picks up the story after Jesus' baptism and describes how two of John's disciples, one of whom was Andrew, Simon Peter's brother, spoke to Jesus, asking him where he lived. Jesus said, "Come and see," and, immediately, Andrew became a disciple of Jesus. Then he found his brother, telling him, "We have found the Messiah," and Peter went with him to Jesus and became a disciple of Christ when Jesus said to him, "You are Simon son of John; you are to be called Cephas" (meaning Rock). The next day Philip and Nathanael were recruited and, after that, John tells about Jesus' first miracle at the wedding at Cana in Galilee, when he turned water into wine as the first sign that he was the Messiah.

Matthew says the Holy Spirit led Jesus into the wilderness after he was baptized by John at the River Jordan; he spent forty days there and was severely tempted by Satan. When he returned from that experience, he moved to the lakeside town of Capernaum and began to preach, almost in the manner of John the Baptizer, "Repent, for the kingdom of heaven is close at hand." As he walked by the shore of the Sea of Galilee, he saw two fishermen, Simon and Andrew, and invited them, "Follow me, and I will make you fishers of men." They immediately followed Jesus without any questions or protestations. Shortly afterward, Jesus came upon two other fishermen, James and John, and called to them to follow. They, too, did just that. And great crowds were attracted by his preaching, without the hype and hoopla of some modern-day evangelists who bus people into their meetings from, sometimes, hundreds of miles away. So, says Matthew, began the ministry of Jesus to the people of Galilee. Initially, it was successful indeed.

The two stories are different, but one thing is the same in both of them; it has to do with the recruitment of the disciples by Jesus. It was radically different from modern recruiting methods; Jesus was the catalyst in the procedure. His personality, his message, the personal dynamism of the Son of God, and the authoritative figure he must have been attracted people so completely they dropped everything and followed him. There was no involved interview, no presentation of qualifications, no job analysis by Jesus, but simply a "follow me" — and they did. Anyone who has applied for a job today knows such procedures would never work. The recruitment of employees is complex and often time-consuming in the church, as well as in the world, whether it concerns parish pastors or seminary professors. Just recently, a friend of mine applied for what would probably be a temporary position in a seminary of a different denomination; he is Lutheran and the seminary is Roman Catholic. The job interview was a two-day process in which, among other things, he had to teach two preaching classes, lecture to professors and students, as well as participate in a lengthy personal interview. He says it was rigorous, despite the fact that it was for a temporary position. He did get the position, which made it worthwhile (and the job might be extended). Anyone who has participated in the call process of a pastor today, knows that the calling of a parish pastor is just as thorough and rigorous a procedure as the hiring of a seminary professor, or even a person in business or industry. Preparing for and going through interviews has almost become a science for personnel people and for those seeking employment. Jesus, however, simply looked at Peter and Andrew, James and John, and said, "Follow me." That just wouldn't do today. But the methodology worked for Jesus, according to the story told by the evangelists.

Jesus knew the kind of people he was looking for and, when he saw them, he singled them out and made an immediate decision about their fitness to be his disciples. He was a great judge of character, but he also could accurately estimate the potential of people to grow and become the kind of people needed for Christian ministry. That isn't always easy to do. Fitness and aptitude can't always be determined by a battery of academic and psychological tests; personal interviews and assessments, supported by academic records and letters of recommendation, need to be put alongside the tests for one's fitness, even for entrance and, later, matriculation at a theological school.

The disciples Jesus chose wouldn't be able to gain entrance to a theological school today, because they wouldn't have the academic background, let alone the culture and knowledge of the world and people required of theological students of this era. They had no formal education, and it is highly unlikely they knew much about the world; they were improbable candidates for ministry. What a loss it would have been to Christ and the Church, had they been unable to qualify to follow Jesus.

Aside from such considerations, Jesus was asking for trouble when he failed to tell them what they would be doing, when he neglected to give them a kind of job description. Some of the trouble that occurred later on, such as their arguments over who was the greatest among them, might have stemmed from the lack of a job description. Such a procedure today would be deemed inexcusable; no person qualified for a particular position in industry, education, the public sector, or the church would accept a position for which there was no job description. It is simply an inappropriate way to do things, and trouble will surely come in time. Promising careers have been destroyed simply because misunderstanding occurred over responsibilities connected to a job or a position. Lives have been shattered and suicides have resulted from failure to meet expectations that were never spelled out.

There were times, of course, when things got tough, especially toward the end of Jesus' ministry when it appeared he was totally wrong about the disciples he had chosen. One of them betrayed him, Peter denied him, and all except John deserted him in his time of trial. Three years with Jesus doesn't seem to have matured them in the faith. That was a training period for the disciples, a three-year internship, if you will, intended to prepare them so they could carry on and effectively preach the Gospel and organize the church after Jesus' earthly life was terminated. Calvin Stanley, who is now ten years old, was born blind; he has congenital glaucoma and will never see. But his mother, Ethel, is a remarkable woman who accepted his blindness when he was quite young and determined to do all she could to enable him to get along on his own in the world. She has not worked since Calvin was born and has acquired the ability to be an extraordinary teacher. "Child," she once told him, "one day I won't be here and I won't be able to pick you up — so you have to try to be something on your own. You have to learn to deal with this (blindness), and to do that, you have to learn how to think." She has been teaching him how to live and think for the past ten years and, apparently, has helped him become a whole and independent human being.[37] Jesus had only three years to prepare his disciples for the day when they would be on their own and have to carry on the communication of the Gospel without him.

It wasn't until after Jesus' resurrection that the world could comprehend how well Jesus had chosen his disciples and how thorough their training had been. "Why did Jesus choose me?" Calvin once asked of Ethel Stanley. She answered, "I don't know why, Calvin. Maybe there's a special plan for you in your life and there's a reason for this. But this is the way you're going to be and you can deal with it." The disciples were able to face every difficulty, pass every trial, preach and teach effectively, and even face death as martyrs for the faith after Jesus ascended to the Father, quite in contrast to the sort of people they seem to be in the Gospels. Peter was crucified upside down, according to tradition, Bartholomew was supposed to have been skinned alive, and all the others, with the exception of John, witnessed to the Gospel by laying down their lives for the faith. They not only followed Jesus, when following him might have been a bit of a lark, but they followed him all the way to their crosses; that takes rather extraordinary faith in very unusual people. Jesus' recruiting and training methods weren't up to our standards today, but we know now they were more than adequate in his selection and education of the disciples.

As for the rest of the story about the beginning of Jesus' ministry, the report is that his teaching in the synagogues and his preaching of the gospel were very successful. He also healed "every disease and every infirmity among the people," and his ministry got off to a rousing start. Large crowds followed him wherever he went and countless people were won over to the gospel. It was a remarkable phenomenon for that time, but something that has been seen in other religions, too. In a little over a decade, the Shiite branch of the Muslim faith has risen from an insignificant group to a dominant force in the Mohammedan faith, largely because Iman Moussa Sadr, its spiritual leader, founded the Amal movement in 1974. Amal is the Arabic word for hope, and that is the doctrine preached and taught to the Shiite Muslims by Moussa Sadr and the present leader, Nabir Berri. They have sought to develop in the Shiites "a sense of identity, purpose and belonging." That they have succeeded in this has been seen in their growing influence in Lebanon and the Middle East, and in the important role they are playing in the future of that area of the world. The Shiites have rallied around their leaders in much the same way that the Galileans and others in the Holy Land embraced Jesus and the Christian faith.[38] The similarity between the two ends, more or less, at that point, because the Christian faith is basically concerned with proclaiming the good news of salvation and in seeking freedom and justice for all people. Jesus and his disciples, preached a different sort of good news. That is the next story.

Matthew 5:1-12

Epiphany 4 (C, L)
Ordinary Time 4 (RC)

Training Session

The recruiting of the twelve disciples is now complete. Jesus has chosen a group of unlikely candidates — fishermen, tax collectors, unsophisticated Galileans, and others — to communicate the good news to the world that he is the Messiah. Training these people for their task is the second phase of this operation. Jesus takes the disciples away from the crowds for an educational retreat on the side of a nearby mountain. Their three-year training session begins with a lecture by their teacher and master, Jesus.

Jesus sat down and assumed, by that action, the formal role of the rabbi, the teacher. He could have paced back and forth, or simply stood in one place, but if he walked around, stood, or, alternately, sat and stood, the character of the occasion would have been changed. Jesus wanted the disciples to know the importance of what he was saying to them, so he took the authoritative position of the teacher; he sat down, "opened his mouth, and taught them, saying . . ." What he said had immediate and lasting impact on them, although they didn't fully comprehend the meaning of his words until years later, especially when they got into trouble with the authorities and their lives were threatened. Then they really comprehended what the so-called "Sermon on the Mount" actually means for people who believe Jesus to be the Messiah.

Even though he was opening up his mind and heart to them, and they understood that, it seems like a very limited type of an initial training session. Couldn't he have found some spot in the Temple to teach his disciples? He was not in any real trouble or danger as yet. Or why didn't he take them to a home where they could have had a room to themselves, in which some discussion might have taken place? To sit on a hillside doesn't seem a suitable setting for such an important undertaking. He was about to reveal the secrets of the kingdom of heaven to them! But Jesus had his reasons, one of which was the immediate success of his preaching, as evidenced in the large crowds he attracted and who followed him wherever he went in Galilee. It was a kind of on-the-job training: "You've heard my message to the people, 'Repent, for the kingdom of heaven is at hand,' and you've seen how the people have responded to it; now let me spell out for you the benefits and blessings that accrue for those people who accept what I have preached and have come to believe in me." The message of this training session is almost an answer to people who ask the old question of Jesus, "What's in it for me?" It could be said that the Sermon on the Mount is a product-oriented lesson given by Jesus.

The Christian faith has benefits and blessings; it is the source of genuine joy which cannot be taken away from people by anything that might happen to them. God, we know now, has given us entrance into the kingdom in Jesus Christ through his death and resurrection; he has saved us from sin and death, and that cannot be taken away from us. That, indeed, is the basic reason for being joyful and hopeful: our Savior, Jesus Christ, lives, and we live in him forever! If we believe in him, through the grace of God, there is nothing in life that can detract from our joy or prevent us from living a life that is a benefit and a blessing to others. In 1984, Mr. and Mrs. Dean Kohl raised over $100,000 so their young daughter, Susan, might undergo a liver transplant at the University of Minnesota Hospitals, in an attempt to save her life. She died before a suitable donor-liver could be located and, of course, her parents were shattered by her death. I don't know if they are Christians, but I do know they responded in the way Christians are intended to live; they mourned, but they were comforted in their grief and they determined they would do something to show their gratitude to all the people who had contributed to the fund for Susan. They purchased a former fraternity house on the campus of the University of Minnesota and proceeded to renovate it so it could be used by the parents of other children awaiting organ transplants at that hospital. Transplant House was opened on June 15, 1985, by the Kohls. Dean explained: "It's our way of repaying all the goodness that has been given to us. This is but a small way (of doing this)." A sign outside the house reads: "Welcome to Transplant House," and it really represents a response to the grace given to them by those who made generous contributions to the fund for Susan.[39] Susan died, but the goodness and genuine concern of others, who were able to put themselves into the situation with the Kohls, could not be taken away. That, indeed, is a Christian response, the kind of thing Jesus was talking about in his training session with the disciples.

Nor could their participation in the fund for Susan be taken away from the people who respondad. They, too, were "blessed" by God, not in the sense of gaining riches or worldly goods in return for their monetary gifts, but from the perspective of knowing that in giving they had received a gift from God which gave them lasting joy. A headline in the newspaper announced, " 'We are the World' sponsors see Ethiopa tragedy firsthand;" it was preceded by a film clip on television which showed the singers and performers actually seeing the tragedy on the spot. Harry Belafonte and others toured the refugee camp at Mekelle, Ethiopa, which is essentially a "feeding camp" set up to alleviate some of the hunger and suffering. They helped to pass out biscuits and bread and T-shirts to the children. Marion Jackson said that, despite what they had seen and heard, it is still a shock to discover the extent to which "something like this exists in the world today." A too-little-too-late attitude of utter helplessness and resignation might result from such an experience, simply because some of the people, especially the children, are beyond help. Dr. Irwin Redlener, a pediatrician who heads USA for Africa's medical group, said, "It's an impossible problem. The problem here is that so many of these children have (had) severe malnutrition over an extended period that the hope of recovery in physical development and brain growth is gone." Anyone who saw the picture of Harry Belafonte with one of the near-skeleton children will never forget it. For the sponsors of "We Are the World," there will always be the knowledge they have done something of consequence by entering into the suffering of these people, and that will never be taken away from them. Who can predict what additional good will come out of their experience with that terrible tragedy.[40]

That's the sort of thing Jesus was talking about in the Sermon on the Mount — never-ending joys that cannot be diminished or destroyed by anything that happens in this life, because God has given us entrance into the kingdom and the work of the kingdom here on earth through Jesus Christ. People are genuinely blessed:

When they know they are absolutely dependent upon
God — that they cannot save themselves —
and fully trust God as those who are
"poor in spirit" and live their lives with a
semblance of perfect obedience;

when their hearts are broken for those who
suffer in the world and for their own sin,
which may have contributed to that suffering.
In that suffering, they will find joy;

when they are genuinely "meek," knowing when
to vent their anger at some of the outrageous
situations in life that heap pain and anguish
upon innocent people—and allow God to control
their lives;

when they really "hunger and thirst after
righteousness," as though they are actually
starving and dying of thirst, instead of pursuing
the pleasures and material blessings of
this world, they will be satisfied by God;

when they are able to see matters from the
perspective of others — and act thereon — they are
among the "merciful" because they have comprehended
the nature of God's never-ending mercy
as it is given to the world in Jesus. They have
already received mercy from God;

when they live without guile, have the
motives of the "pure in heart," they
know that they will see God;

when they make peace among people and the
nations of the earth, they become the "children
of God," for that is the way the "children
of God are expected to live;

when they face death for Christ — actually, or in the form of insults and ridicule or other kinds of persecution from the enemies of Christ, they know that God has a place for them in the kingdom of heaven.

And the message to you and me is this: We are the people of the promise, and Jesus was talking about us, too, when he addressed the disciples on the mountainside that day. He has made all of us his own, given us the very blessings of the kingdom — the knowledge that he has saved us, set us free from sin and self, and incorporated us, through baptism, into that kingdom which will have no end. Therefore, we have reason indeed for being continually joyful, because the blessings of the kingdom are ours.

As I write this, two young men are canoeing from the headwaters of the Mississipi River, in Lake Itasca, Minnesota, to New Orleans, a 2200-mile journey, in the hope they can raise a minimum of $10,000 to help stamp out pain, suffering, and hunger in the world. Dan Macauley, one of the two, said, "If everybody does their share, we can wipe out hunger by the end of the century."[41] That might sound like a truism, or it might seem to be a bit naive, but that's the kind of action Christians ought to be engaged in because they have heard and believe the good news about Jesus. It is a way of articulating and communicating the Gospel, according to Jesus, and from the perspective of the Sermon on the Mount. That's living out the joy, the blessedness that God has given us in Christ.

Matthew 5:13-16 (C, RC) | *Epiphany 5 (C, L)*
Matthew 5:13-20 | *Ordinary Time 5 (RC)*

Second Lesson

We're back on the hillside again, and Jesus is still talking to his disciples. The Beatitudes constitute a first lesson, which all hangs together when we look at them and reflect upon them. From the end of the Beatitudes through the next two and a half chapters of Matthew's Gospel, we seem to have fragments from Jesus' three-year teaching ministry that are strung together in didactic disarray.

One wonders, since neither Mark nor John reports anything like the Sermon on the Mount, and although Luke does have a parallel to it in his sermon on the plain, if Jesus actually gave all of this material at one sitting. Could this simply be various of his sayings strung together for Matthew's readers? Most of the "sermon" does appear in individual verses in the other Gospels. Jesus was too good a teacher, it seems to me, to begin the educational retreat as he did and then simply to ramble on and on. What we notice today is the mood changes a bit and Jesus directly addresses the disciples with, "You are the salt of the earth; but if salt has lost its taste, how shall its saltiness be restored?"

That's a saying which has made its way into our everyday lives. Nearly everyone knows somebody who is considered to be "the salt of the earth." A charter plane was about to take off from the airport in Acapulco, Mexico, when a young man dashed up to the gate counter, explaining he was supposed to be on the plane. He shouted: "I've got reservations on that plane and my bags are on it and there isn't another plane I can take. It's a disaster for me if I don't get on that plane . . . Can't you contact them and let them know I'm here? . . . I was here two hours before the flight. I just stepped into the gift shop. They must have called it then." "Senor," answered the man at the gate, "I am sorry but we have no communications with the captain and we cannot stop the flight." In five minutes the plane left and Steve Parenteau, an American junior high school counselor, remained in Acapulco with no baggage, not much money, and the information that another flight would leave in three or four days; it would cost him $800 to take that flight. For four hours, Enrique Magana, the gate attendant, contacted all agencies — "by the book" — that were supposed to help in such situations, but to no avail. The American was out of luck. "The only place I can think of," Magana said, "is my house." For a week, the young counselor from the wealthy Minneapolis suburb, Edina, lived in the modest home on the hill of the Mexican airport worker and his family. He ate at their table, played chess with Enrique, and read books and played with the kids while their mother earned $5 a day as a school teacher. He even "drank the water." Asked, when he got home, how he accounted for the airport worker's act, Steve said, "Some people make a commandment out of manuals and protocol. Others try kindness."[42] People like Enrique Magana are surely "the salt of the earth." At least, Steve Parenteau must think so.

Jesus expected that kind of activity out of his disciples; more than that, he told them they *were* "the salt of the earth." They could give life the special quality that makes it worth living, not only by works of love, mercy, and kindness, by being what Christians are meant to be, but also by communicating the good news to all the people they met. That means, the disciples were "the light of the world." Their faith in Christ and his Word, in that pagan society, were like a beacon guiding a lost ship to safety. Their light could not be hidden, any more than a city on top of a hill could hide in the darkness of the night, so Jesus commanded them: "Let your light so shine before men, that they may see your good works and give glory to your Father who is in heaven."

That's easier said than done. Our lights tend to grow dim or even go out at times. Sometimes the connection to the power source is broken by our negligence and spiritual failures. Years ago, a pastor began his ministry in spectacular fashion in a city where I was serving. He was constantly making headlines and seemed to be attracting many people to the congregation he served. He had all sorts of ideas and innovations, and people were constantly talking about him. His outdoor bulletin board not only announced his sermons with striking titles, but it carried news of each event this pastor had planned. Someone asked the assistant to the bishop of his denomination, "What will happen when he runs out of ideas and gimmicks?" "Oh," came the reply, "I'm sure he will recharge his batteries and come up with some new ideas and programs that will continue to work." He didn't. He couldn't, because he was operating on a superficial level and was not wired into the power source existing in the Word and the Holy Spirit. Before long, he moved on and soon was forgotten.

To be "the light of the world" means we are not simply to shine by ourselves; it is not our brilliance that illuminates the darkness of the world in which we live, but the light that comes from God in Jesus Christ. He was the Light of the World and, if in any measure we become the light of the world, it can only be through the power he makes available to us. That power-source has to be tapped regularly; we must be connected to it or our light will go out. One Father's Day, my son's family gave me a flashlight as an appropriate gift. They know I love to fish at night, occasionally, and they believed this to be a useful gift for that reason. Our home, too, is in an area where we have a lot of summer outages of electricity; a good flashlight is a necessity, and they knew that, too. The flashlight they gave me is no ordinary light; it is rechargeable. But it doesn't have a bracket that has to be mounted on the wall, nor does it have any wiring. The prongs that fit into an electrical outlet fold down into the flashlight — a neat little unit. It gives excellent light, as long as it is charged up. But if its power is used up and it is not plugged in regularly, it gives little or no light and soon goes out. We cannot be, any more than could the disciples, "the light of the world" by ourselves; we need to be connected to Christ, as the disciples were, to shine forth so people will see God in Jesus Christ.

Jesus also made it quite clear to them that their life-styles could either enhance their "light" or detract from it in the eyes of people whom they met and to whom they preached. Christian freedom doesn't mean believers can live any way they want to, do anything that pleases them; that is the way of the world, not the way of God. Jesus told the disciples, "Think not that I have come to abolish the law and the prophets; I have come not to abolish them but to fulfill them." He did that by his perfect obedience to the law of God, which cost him his life on the cross, and by giving new meaning to the law in his teaching. Those who flaunt God's law are definitely treading in dangerous territory and, sooner or later, they will pay a price for their transgressions. I once knew a man who was completely taken in by "situation ethics." He liked to talk about Christian freedom as a divine mandate to do anything, particularly in the area of marital relationships. "Free love and affairs are totally appropriate," he would argue, adding, "for everyone but my wife and daughters." Those who knew him thought he was just trying to be provocative in his comments, until he got involved with a woman and the news got back to his wife and family. He paid a bitter price for his one-time infidelity. After he was forgiven, he did come to realize that freedom from the law means Christians have been delivered from fulfilling the law to gain their salvation; only Jesus could do that. Freedom from the law does not mean Christians are free to live as they please. We may have forgotten that today, in this secular age that differs from Jesus' time, because Christian life-style was radically different then from the way non-Christians lived. Can you tell the difference between Christians and non-Christians by the way they live? I must admit that I can't all of the time.

Jesus' disciples, therefore, were told to be reconcilers, bringing together, not separating, people in the community envisioned by God and made real by Jesus Christ in his body, the church. People who are at odds with one another are not fit for the company of God or his community on earth; they damage and destroy it, thereby doing harm to the entire Christian endeavor. One of the privileges that comes to a professor is to be appointed vice-pastor of a vacant congregation by the bishop. A few years ago I was serving in such a capacity. The preaching went reasonably well, as did the other daily affairs of the parish, but the church council meetings were something of a problem. It was evident there were two rival factions in the congregation, and two men on the church council were the leaders and spokespersons for the different groups. They were restrained at the first few meetings I attended, but finally got into an argument, at a later meeting, that almost became a fight. I was afraid they would go out behind the church building and engage in a really bitter argument or even exchange blows, so I tried to defuse the controversy by saying, "Let's look at all sides of this question before we make any decision." It stopped the near-argument of the two men, and other people entered into the discussion. The strange thing was the two were not as far apart on the question as they thought they were, and when they saw that, they laughed and actually went out and had coffee together and became friends again. When I finished my stint as vice-pastor of the congregation, the secretary of the church council sent a letter to me in which she said, in part, "Thank you for acting as peace-maker in our church council meetings." I had forgotten all about that incident and the rather insignificant thing I had said until she reminded me of it. I learned again what people may do if they try to be peacemakers in the name of Jesus Christ. It is the key to reconciliation among people and integral to the ministry of those, lay persons or clergy, who would preach and teach and effectively communicate the Gospel to the world.

On second thought, it may be that these four different sayings of Jesus not only hang together, but that they are integral to each other and vital to our ministries today. He has made us "the salt of the earth," "the light of the world," and has gained freedom from the fulfillment of the law for us by his perfect sacrifice, thereby reconciling us to God and to each other. That's the heart of our ministry, so let's get on with it.

Matthew 5:17-26 (C)
Matthew 5:20-37 (L)
Matthew 5:17-37 (RC)

Epiphany 6 (C, L)
Ordinary Time 6 (RC)

The Importance of Forgiving Others

Archbishop's Easter Message, read the headlines for one newspaper on Easter Monday, 1986, followed by a sub-heading in larger print, "Runcie applauds forgiving vicar." The reporter, Clifford Longley, wrote, "The Archbishop of Canterbury, Dr. Robert Runcie, yesterday bestowed an Easter absolution on the perpetrators of the recent horrific incident in a west London vicarage." Longley was referring to the attack upon a Church of England clergyman, his daughtar, and her boy friend that occurred in the middle of Lent. The vicar received a fractured skull, the other young man was badly beaten, and the vicar's daughter was raped. When the vicar recovered and preached his first sermon, he called upon his congregation to forgive the people who had done this terrible act, just as he had done. That's why the Archbishop of Canterbury had spoken about the vicar in his sermon; he was preaching about forgiveness, in general, and showing his hearers how the Easter message, specifically, applies to life today.

The purpose of Jesus' mission two thousand years ago was to bring about reconciliatian between God and his people and between all people on the earth. He began his ministry by proclaiming, "Repent, for the kingdom of heaven is near." And now, in his Sermon on the Mount, our Lord adds a warning, "For I tell you that unless your righteousness exceeds that of the Pharisees and the teachers of the law, you will certainly not enter the kingdom of heaven." One could get the impression that reconciliation with God depends upon the good works which people do in their daily lives, couldn't one? It sounds as though Jesus is making it almost impossible for ordinary people to become reconciled to God and enter into the kingdom, doesn't it? Who could surpass the "righteousness of the Pharisees"? They tried to obey every detail of God's Law. How could anyone improve upon the religious life of the Pharisees? Heaven — and reconciliation with God — are out of the reach of most of us, aren't they?

And, of course, there is no way that we can earn our way into the kingdom of God, no matter how much good we do or how dedicated we may be to Christ and his church here on earth. Our sin separates us from the Father, and only Jesus could do anything about that; there is no way that we can gain our own forgiveness of sins. That's why the Cross was necessary; the sinless Son of God had to offer himself to God as a sacrifice for sin and, thereby, attain forgiveness — salvation — and deliverance from the consequences of sin. "The Road to Reconciliation," as someone has called Jesus' death on Calvary, is the only way that we can get into the kingdom of heaven. We must never forget that old hymn:

There was no other good enough
To pay the price of sin;
He only could unlock the gate
of heaven, and let us in.

One mighty act by Jesus — not a thousand good deeds on our part — gains us access to "the mercy seat." And Jesus doesn't want us to forget it: "Unless your righteousness surpasses that of the Pharisees" means something quite different than it seems to mean, doesn't it? It has to do with forgiving those who have wronged us, bestowing upon them the gift that can never be earned or deserved — forgiveness — because forgiveness is always a gift of grace from God to us and from each of us to one another. What, then, was Jesus getting at when he said, "Unless your righteousness . . ."?

For one thing, it is necessary that we comprehend that forgiveness is God's gift of love and grace in Jesus Christ — and never forget this central truth of the Christian faith. It is God's way — the only way open to him — of restoring us to communion with himself; he *gave* Jesus Christ to suffering and death out of love. He reconciled us to himself in Christ and saved us from sin and death;

he has restored us to what we were in the beginning, people who were made in the "image of God." Gustav Wingren tells us that reconciliation has to do with restoration of fallen humanity to a state of grace: "Salvation means that the human being again becomes truly human."

It took another act of creation — a new creation in Jesus' death and resurrection — to accomplish that restoration to grace, and that was done by God — on our behalf — in his gift to, and for, the world, Jesus Christ, our Lord.

Jesus also wants us to remember that, when we have accepted his gift of grace, forgiveness, that we must pass that gift along to all people who have done us harm or hurt. "Forgive us our sins, as we forgive those who sin against us" is a petition of prayer that we had better back up with deeds that are the consequence of being forgiven by God, because we forfeit God's gift of forgiveness and reconciliation *if* we, in our turn, fail to forgive those who have wronged us in any way. But that's so hard to do, isn't it? And it is such a rare occurrence, even in the Christian community. That's why Archbishop Runcie grounded his sermon in his use of the story about the London vicar, his daughter, and their friend: "We have seen a fine and impressive example of this quiet Easter faith (that we have been forgiven by God in Jesus' death and resurrection) shining through personal tragedy in a Christian congregation," and he adds, "Such heroic healing power could hardly fail to move the most determined cynic." The Archbishop may or may not be correct in his conclusion about the impact of this event on cynics and unbelievers, but he surely is right in calling this an "impressive example of ... quiet Easter faith." They have God's gift, and they keep it by passing forgiveness on to others who like ourselves do not deserve it. The gift — forgiveness — must be bestowed on others by those who claim they have received it — or reconciliation with God and entrance into the kingdom are forfeited.

But, you and I often object, Jesus lived in a different era and in a totally different kind of world than we live in. Injustice and violence and all kinds of terrorism constantly threaten our well-being and our very existence. How can we forgive the terrorist who plants a bomb under the seat of an airliner and blows four people to their deaths? How can we say to Kurt Waldheim, who after serving as Secretary General of the United Nations for ten years is now accused of being a Nazi war criminal (if the accusations are true),

"We forgive you"? How can we offer forgiveness to someone who has cheated or hurt us and, perhaps, has done us irreparable harm? Everywhere in the world, Dr. Runcie claims, "we are confronted by the dark demonic dimension of human nature which can cause the most resilient spirit to quiver and quake. As we watch or read the news we are constantly sickened by the sights or first-hand accounts of violence against women and children, against whole groups of people who are labeled and despised. The sickness is in the hearts and minds of men and children." So, we say of such people, "They don't deserve to belong to the human race. And we refuse to forgive them. And, too, we place ourselves in jeopardy of losing God's precious gift in Christ — forgiveness and reconciliation and heaven itself — when we do this sort of thing.

Stanley Spencer, the Scottish painter who died a quarter of a century ago, makes us realize that we would rather judge and condemn other persons rather than forgive them. Despite the fact that he could hardly be numbered among those who confess that Christ is Lord (he never affiliated himself with any denomination or communion), he spent much of his life painting scenes from the Passion of Jesus Christ. He did them in a style that is reminiscent of Gaugin — large, exaggerated, rather primitive types of people. Late in his career, he was accused of painting obscene scenes and, accordingly, was refused membership in The Royal Academy (of art). And his second wife, Priscilla, made it impossible for him to obtain a divorce, which made it impossible for him to remarry his first wife, Hilda, whom he really seemed to love. One of his last paintings about Jesus' Passion demonstrates that he never forgave The Royal Academy, the man who had betrayed him to the Academy, the common people who criticized his work and accepted his "condemnation," and Priscilla. In "Christ Delivered to the People," Spencer shows his hatred and his refusal to forgive these people by making them the enemies of Jesus Christ in this painting. He believed that he was betrayed as Christ was, but he could not say, with Christ, "Father, forgive them, for they know not what they do."

"Christ Delivered to the People" has Christ in the center of the painting, being shoved and pulled toward Calvary by a variety of people. Judas Iscariot, soldiers, common people, even two children pull on his clothing. Pilate sits in a corner of the picture, wearing a fool's cap, washing his hands before a servant, who is meant to represent the common people. Pilate stands for The Royal

Academy. Judas is given a face that could only be that of the man who had betrayed him. He gave the hairdo of Priscilla to a woman who stands to the side of the procession and seems to be affirming what is happening to him. He pictures the eleven disciples shrinking away in the background, just as he believed that his painter-friends and colleagues had abandoned him, too. "Christ Delivered to the People" is a kind of self-portrait, simply because it seems to reveal the character of Spencer and his refusal — to his dying day — to forgive the people whom he counted as his enemies. And isn't that a picture of us, too, at our worst? "Unless your righteousness surpasses that of the Pharisees" by sharing the gift of forgiveness with others, "you will certainly not enter the kingdom of heaven." There's a bit of Spencer's unforgiving spirit in us, too, isn't there?

Does this mean that, to be counted among the forgiven because we forgive those who hurt and harm us, that we are to turn our backs on all forms of evil in the world and let evil have its way? Are we simply to say to thieves and robbers, terrorists and murderers, as well as all those other people who prove to be our enemies by what they do to us, "we forgive you, no matter what you may have done — or will do to people,"as though sin and evil are of no consequence? Christians must be the foes of all kinds of vicious assaults, every form of violence, callous cruelty, persecution, poverty, and powerlessness, according to Archbishop Runcie — and, of course, according to Jesus, too!

Another current headline next to the article about Runcie's sermon, reads, "Soldier shot at ceremony (in Ireland)," while the next two columns are introduced by this headline: "Police hunt death squad Libyans." In both cases, those who perpetrated deeds of terrorism are being sought out; if arrested, they will be tried and, if convicted, punished for their evil deeds. Such procedures are necessary and must be supported by Christians, if there is to be any semblance of peace and harmony in the world. Innocent people have to be protected from those who would do them harm.

But the workings of legal machinery don't eliminate the need for offering forgiveness to the people who have wronged us or others. We can, and must, say, with King Arthur to Guenivere, "Lo, I forgive thee, as the eternal God forgives." And we must mean it! That's exactly what the vicar in London did, because the people who had attacked him, his daughter, and the young man — and robbed them, too — had been apprehended and were facing trial when he preached his "forgiveness" sermon.

"Are we losing the war on violence?" That's a question that is being seriously asked. It must be faced head on in our times. It has been said that "Everybody knows that society is getting more and more violent, and that individual acts of violence have almost doubled in ten years, crime has been described as "a growth industry" by one law officer. Christians, it is being said more and more, must participate in the restoration of a sick society, not merely by calling for legal measures to counter crime, but by participating actively in projects that rescue and renew people who are being oppressed. We can find ways to support the blacks and Indian minorities who are being persecuted in South Africa; pressure upon politicians to develop economic sanctions against South Africa is one way to participate in this battle for the liberation of persecuted people. We may have to engage in direct confrontation of evil when we see it, but remember that this might put us — one way or another — alongside Christ on the Cross. Forgiveness, if we get to the roots of evil in our world. may be quite costly should we dare to follow Christ in helping others and healing the wounds of people in the world.

Just a few waeks ago, my wife, daughter, granddaughter, and I visited a couple of people in Edinburgh, Scotland, whom we (not including my granddaughter) had not seen for 21 years. Dr. and Mrs. Joseph Been moved to Edinburgh from South Africa 22 years ago; we became acquainted with them immediately upon their arrival and, through my wife's gift for communicating with people, have kept up the friendship that began when we met them. They were forced to leave South Africa, despite the fact that Dr. Been came from a prominent family in Rostenberg; Joe's father was one of the founding fathers of the town (two of his physician brothers and one brother who is a dentist still live there). Clarice Been was an active member of the Black Sash. She also allowed her black servant's husband to live on their compound; she entertained Indians living in South Africa in her home. The Beens had a lovely home. It was only five years old when life became unbearable for them. In the belief that they had done all they could do at that time, and also to protect their four children from recriminations by the authorities and other people, they sold their home; Dr. Been gave up his practice, and they moved to Edinburgh. There they had to start all over again — and they did so gladly. Joe and Clarica Been are Jewish, but the sacrifices they have made for the downtrodden of South Africa are worthy of any Christian saint. Carrying the cross of Christ into a world of violence and hatred, so as to correct the wrongs and heal the wounds of those who have been victimized in various ways, can be a costly business.

The human thing (which is really the *inhuman* thing) to do when we have been wronged by others is to get even with them. But Christ has established a different pattern for our lives: forgiveness, "Unless your righteousnass surpasses that of the Pharisees, you will certainly not enter into the kingdom of heaven." Our business as Christians, whatever shape the details of Christian discipleship may assume, is to forgive others as we have been forgiven and reconciled to God in Jesus Christ. "Though Christianity had to be concerned with opposing social injustices, its main message was this forgiveness, offered through Christ," Dr. Runcie declared to his congregation and the world. This part of the Sermon on the Mount is connected to Calvary, "the Mount of Forgiveness and Reconciliation," where God worked out our salvation in Jesus Christ. And we dare never forget it, so that we may retain the precious gift — reconciliation with God — which he has obtained for us all.

Matthew 5:27-37 (see Epiphany 6)
Matthew 5:38-48 (L, RC)

Epiphany 7 (C, L)
Ordinary Time 7 (RC)

Cross Work

Jesus might have been loving, kind, and good, but he wasn't very practical. As he closes out this first section of the Sermon on the Mount, it is pure Gospel we hear today that supercedes the law of last week. And Jesus shows us just how impractical the Gospel actually is. He instructs the disciples and us, to:

offer no resistance to wicked people who
might hurt or offend you;
turn the other cheek if someone hits you
on one side of the face;
give your coat as well as your shirt to
anyone who asks;
go farther than you have to when you are
pressed into service by someone;
respond generously to everyone who asks for
financial help or a loan.

Those maxims are surely lovely to contemplate in one's mind, but it would be totally ridiculous to live according to them. From the perspective of the world we live in, they don't make much sense at all.

This world seems to be filled with ruthless robbers, murderers, rapists, and terrorists, in addition to a few good people:

The wicked man will stop at nothing, given resistance, or not.
. . .I read an account of a robbery in a nursing home.
A thief entered the room of two elderly women and ripped

their wedding and engagement rings off their fingers. Both of them received cuts on their fingers, and one was cut above the eye and around the mouth. One lady had a one carat diamond engagement ring and a gold wedding band with diamonds in it stolen from her finger. The two of them might have been killed if they had resisted. The police captain, who commented upon the crime, said, "I am appalled by this type of crime." Who isn't?

Defy a mugger and he may just kill you.Thus, Bernard Getz became a hero when he gunned down the four young men who accosted him on the New York subway train. Just asking him for money was a life-threatening request, as far as he was concerned, so he went into action as a vigilante and wound up in court instead of being a victim of the muggers. Robert Stethem, the young sailor on the TWA flight that was highjacked in June of 1985, discovered that non-resistance does not pay off; the highjackers beat him, and shot him in the head, and then threw his body out of the airplane onto the tarmac in Beirut.

The condition of the world in which we live seems to demand that we take personal action in response to the different kinds of threats we face:

Give in to those who offend you before they do whatever was intended in the first place. The terrorists and others have taught us that, and retaliation could very well become the order of the day in contemporary life. *Time* told about the arrest of seven seniors and one junior at Pascal High School in Fort Worth, Texas; they belonged to the Legion of Doom, "a society supposedly dedicated to purifying the campus of drug users and petty thieves." Four or more of them also belonged to an organization called the Ambassadors, who patrolled the campus and told others to attend classes; this group was disbanded. The Legion of Doom was made up of young people from "prominent families, (who) prowled less well-to-do neighborhoods at night, firing shots at one student's home, exploding a pipe bomb on another's car. A fire bomb tossed at a black student's house failed to hurt anyone only because it fell short and ignited in the front yard." *Time* reports that one classmate said:"These pillars of our community (were) doing worse things than we will ever do in our lives."

That's what can happen when people attempt to right wrongs done to them by others through violent acts and vigilante efforts. Those who are threatened or hurt can easily get caught up in actions that make matters worse than they were. A course of retaliation simply compounds a wrong and turns the people who are offended into persons who are no better than the ones who did wrong in the first place. Here's where the Gospel of Jesus comes into and touches our lives.

"Love your enemies" — who can do that? This much is clear: Jesus did, even though he could get angry enough with them to condemn their unholy activities. He even loved those who were responsible for his suffering and death. He might not have liked them, or anything about them, but he loved them as children of God; that sort of love is not a feeling, but an act of the will and the mind. It results in beneficial actions on the part of the person who is offended. This is the person whose quality of life is extraordinary, because there is no preoccupation with self, but only a concern for the welfare and improvement of the conditon of others. We call these people "saints" because they have, in some mystifying manner, been able to live out their lives as Christ lived his, even under the most trying and difficult circumstances.

I am fascinated by the city of Rome, partly because it is inhabited by the spirits of the saints who died there as they attempted to live out the Gospel. Wherever a person goes in that city, there are reminders — churches, statues, paintings, and other works of art — that speak of the saints who "loved their enemies" more than they loved themselves. Of the saints of old, Romano Guardini, a Roman Catholic theologian, has this to say: "They knew from their own experience the limitations of paganism — how in spite of its great culture and refinement, one remained a prisoner of the forces of nature; how despite the fantastic intellectual and artistic achievements of paganism, it offered little consolation to the distressed and lonely human heart; how, the beautiful poetic myths and fables of paganism notwithstanding, relatively little was done to satisfy the profound human aspiration for truth and liberty." Through the

Gospel of Jesus, says Guardini, "They were, quite simply, living a new kind of existence ruled by God who was also their King and their Saint."

Not far from the commuter train that takes people into the city from the suburb of EUR, just outside the walls of Rome, there is a spot called Tre Fontana (Three Fountains); three chapels dedicated to St. Paul stand there, because this is the spot where he was beheaded. Legend has it that when his head struck the ground, three springs of water gushed forth and have continued to flow to this day.[46] That's why they named the place Three Fountains, but it is a viable symbol of Paul's love of Christ and the Gospel that compelled him to go into all of the known world preaching the Gospel to all people and telling them, in a sense, "God loves you," and by his deeds, "I love you, too." Almost everywhere one goes in the ancient city, there are reminders of the living and loving spirits of the Christians of that incredible way of life offered to the world by Jesus Christ. They loved their enemies enough to die for them, as Jesus did, and not simply to guarantee their own salvation. Truly, that is living a new kind of life, the Christian life.

And, amazingly, innumerable Christians have followed the example of their Lord, as well as his teachings, when faced with persecution and death. They repeated Jesus' first word on the cross, "Father, forgive them, for they know not what they do," not as a mechanical response to the command of Christ, but as a genuine expression of their love and concern for their enemies. It has been said that nothing dissipates hatred and ill will like prayer does; it makes love possible, hatred impossible. It takes us a long time to learn that, just as it did Russell H. Conwell, the founder of the Baptist Temple, Temple University, and other related institutions in Philadelpia. When he left his home in Massachusetts as a captain in the militia during the Civil War, he was followed by a young boy, Johnny Ring, who idolized him as a swash-buckling sort of local hero. When Johnny was discovered, he begged Conwell to let him stay as his orderly; reluctantly, Captain Conwell did as he requested. But the first night there was trouble, because the boy took out his Bible and began to read it in the presence of the captain, who was an atheist. Conwell ordered him out of the tent if he wanted to read Scripture and pray, but the sixteen-year-old boy simply said, "I will pray for you, Captain." That was the first in a series of incidents, including the death of Johnny Ring, while saving the captain's dress sword which had been given him by their townspeople and which led to the conversion of the atheistic lawyer into a committed Christian and a dedicated and inspired minister of the Gospel.[47] It is impossible to hate those who insult you, injure you, even kill you, if you pray for them; Jesus proved the truth of what he taught on the cross.

Christians are not merely to look in amazement and adoration at the cross of Christ; they are to do the work of Christ. "Cross Work" is as good a name for it as any, because the cross of Christ, while always a symbol of evil and hatred on one hand, will forever be the sign of love, forgiveness, and reconciliation between all people, as well as between God and humanity. The Word made visible in works of love may be the only thing we can do to change things around in this world intent on destroying itself and all of the people in it. This is the road Christians must travel in life, if they are to be "perfect as their Father in heaven is perfect."

Matthew 5:38-48 (C: see Epiphany 7) | *Epiphany 8 (C, L)*
Matthew 6:24-34 (L, RC) | *Ordinary Time 8 (RC)*

Christians Trust in God

One of the most fascinating chapters in Loren Eisele's autobiography, *All the Strange Hours (The Excavation of a Life),* is called "The Ghost World." It is the story of a near tragedy in Eisele's life when he was beginning his career as a professor at the University of Pennsylvania. He awakened one night and discovered he was "running a fever and babbling a lecture to some unseen audience. "Slowly," he writes, "as my consciousness steadied, I grew aware of something strange. Outside, lightning bolts sporadically split the dark. I could see through the bedroom window a torrential rain in progress. After each stroke of lightning I waited for the following thunder. There was none. I was deaf. The last lines were going down. I was alone with that knowledge in the dark."

Eisele had two concerns which gave him reason to fear and worry over the future of his life. He became an insomniac when his father died of cancer; unconsciously, he feared he would contract cancer and die the same way, but he was, on a deeper level, afraid of death. His other fear came from his mother's physical malady; she was stone deaf, and he had observed his mother seemed to be insane, at times. Both parents were dead by the time he began teaching at the University of Pennsylvania, but these two fears were still embedded deeply in his subconscious mind. When he said, "The last lines were going down," he was articulating one, if not both, of these fears, and he entered into a period of worry and despondency that threatened to destroy him.

The physician, whom Eisele and his wife consulted, quickly came to a conclusion: "He needs a specialist," and made arrangements for them to see one that afternoon. Eisele writes: "We went home to wait. I wanted to be alone. I wandered down to the little brook where a faint November light played upon the ripples. I sat on a stump and threw a stone in the water. I thought of those derelicts, including myself, who had similarly waited in the Kansas City (railroad) yards (when he had been a hobo) so long ago, the men cast off by the city, sitting with hands gripping and ungripping, or throwing cinders at a barrel. All those sweating years of danger and effort. If I had not come here this might never have happened. I might still be sitting in another hobo jungle. A tuning fork (usad by the physician) whose vibrations not even the bone would pick up had clarified this. My God, the nerve *must* be gone. 'Face it, face it, face it. You're never going to hear again.' The tortured, straining features of my mother came back to me. How long before I turned paranoid, before . . .''[48]

Sooner or later, most of us have good reasons, from our personal perspective, to fear life or death so much that we are almost paralyzed by worry over our future. Despondency becomes a deep pit, with sheer walls, from which we cannot escape; we become virtual prisoners of fear and worry and may be immobilized by this combination of emotions and the mind. The trouble with any type of overwhelming concern is that it may make emotionally handicapped people of us, who are unable to live normal, productive lives. When we ought to be trusting God and pursuing life to the utmost, we find ourselves being consumed by forces in our lives that are just too much for us to handle. Fear and worry may literally destroy us, or cause us to destroy ourselves, and they are absolutely catastrophic to our relationship to God and people and our growth into mature people of God. Jesus knew that faith in God or the lack of it may be the root of our predicament, and taught, as part of his sermon on the mountainside, "No one can serve two masters; for either he will hate the one and love the other, or he will be devoted to the one and despise the other. You cannot serve God and mammon."

Would Jesus say the same things to us today that he said to the disciples — "do not be anxious about your life, what you shall eat or what shall you drink, nor about your body, what you shall put on. Is not life more than food, and the body more than clothing?" — in the face of the terrible economic chaos, drought, and starvation that are taking so many lives in Africa and other parts of the world? Would he declare, "Therefore do not be anxious about tomorrow, for tomorrow will be anxious for itself. Let the day's own trouble be sufficient for the day,'' when international terrorism may be taking the civilized world into a new era of danger from the nuclear bomb? The American military has perfected a fifty-eight pound nuclear mini-bomb that is almost as powerful as the bomb dropped on Hiroshima. Is it just a matter of time until terrorists obtain such a device and pose an even worse threat to our cities and our life? Isn't this an age in which all of us are entitled to be anxious and to worry about the future? Only a fool would dismiss some of the dangers of life today.

Wasn't Jesus very much in touch with reality and the world of his day? What would he say today?

I am positive he would still tell people, ''Your heavenly Father knows that you need them all (food, clothing, shelter, medical care, and so on). But seek first his (God's) kingdom and his righteousness, and all these things will be yours as well.'' Wasn't he talking about trusting that God would provide us with the opportunities and the resources to obtain the necessities of life, not simply handing us what we need on a platter? Trusting God liberates us from those fears and anxieties which paralyze and immobilize us in daily life. I heard Pastor Paul Peterson (Gloria Dei Church, St. Paul) tell the story of what happened to him when he was taken prisoner by the Germans in World War II. He said, in part: ''I wonder if there is any one here today who has shared with me the loss of freedom, and has been confined against their will in a prison. The forty years that have slid by have thankfully dimmed some of the pain that I experienced when, as a twenty-year old captive of enemy forces, I was consigned to spend some months behind the barbed wire of a prison camp . . . To live your life totally at the whim of your captor is a frightening and painful experience. To be dependent entirely on the grim grace of your captor for a slab of bread or a cup of gruel, or for shelter from the winter is a terrifying thing. We huddled around contraband radios, trying to catch the news that would tell us how near or how far our liberators were from our position.'' As dreadful as their conditions were in that prison camp, he and his friends never lost hope: ''We never doubted for an instant that we would be finally free from the threat of death. Free from hunger. Free from the literally lousy conditions in which we lived in which there was seldom enough water to wash our hands, let alone take a bath.'' That's the kind of trust which we are to have in God, because it is a liberating force in our lives, enabling us to think, to plan, to act and do what has to be done every day that we live.

For Paul Peterson and the other prisoners, their trust freed them from losing hope, from being consumed by bitterness and hatred of their captors and the conditions in which they were forced to exist, even from the fear of death in that prison camp. And they could have a future with hope, as Peterson writes: "But strangely, this (the conditions of their imprisonment) is not my sharpest recollection of those dreadful days. Our shared conversations seldom dwelt on our agony or the injustice of our captors. Rather, our time was spent more often reflecting on what we would do when we got out of our confinement. I think Florence (his wife) still has tucked away little lists I made on the back of dirty scraps of paper of the things I wanted to do when I got home. Tough top sergeants became culinary experts, trading outlandish recipes and menus. And filtering between the food-talk were stories of trips planned or trips past, of families and friends and wives and sweethearts, and all the things we would do when . . ." Because they were able to trust in the might of the American military forces and God, too, they were able to ward off the paralysis of mind and body that comes to people who are imprisoned by fear and worry, and to believe and hope they would be freed to return home to normal lives.[49]

Jesus believed that trusting in God, seeking his kingdom and his righteousness above everything else, will liberate us from imprisonment by anxiety, worry, and fear. Trusting in God frees us so we can use our hearts, minds, and strength to do all those things that need to be done to support our lives and to help others meet their daily needs, too. Trusting in God is our response to the faith-knowledge that he cares about us and all people, and is concerned about our physical welfare and the quality of our lives. But trusting in God is not simply sitting idly, watching the world go by, and waiting for God to do something to help us and others; it is responding to the opportunities we have to do something for others and for ourselves in the name of Jesus Christ. Romano Guardino, when talking about saints in daily life, writes: "There are possibilities in us which could lead us ever farther, out beyond the horizons, to a place where we would have to start over and over again the process of clarifying our intentions, removing afterthoughts and shedding light on interior dodges and dishonesties, conquering the rebellion and meanness in our hearts. There are the possibilities of which Christ has spoken in his "All: all the heart, all the soul, all the strength . . . If we were to probe a little further, . . . we would be able to recognize the outlines of the figure of a new type of saint. It is no longer a matter of a man or woman who does exceptional things, but simply of one who does what every man and woman who wishes to act well in a given situation will do. No more, and no less. Above all, however, this man acts in the perspective of God's will. He understands the task which presents itself to him here and now is indeed something which he must accomplish. He is not a visionary, neither is he a slouch. He makes use of his intelligence to do his duty before God and can give a good reason at all times for what he does . . . His actions are placed in the world, but are subject to the will of God who is the Creator of the world and yet in His Infinity outside it . . . To desire these things: that is true love," and is truly, as Jesus put it, "seeking the kingdom of God and his righteousness."[50]

Those who trust in God above everything else don't worry needlessly about food, clothing, and shelter; they find ways of supplying them to others, as well as obtaining them for themselves. They put those things that they might worry inordinately about in a different perspective — God's, not merely a human point of view — and often discover new ways of doing what has to be done. That's how it was with Loren Eiseley. He writes: "Sitting alone at the kitchen table I tried to put into perspective the fears that still welled up frantically from my long ordeal. I had done a lot of work on (an) article (which his publisher had turned over to another scientist), but since my market was gone, why not attempt a more literary venture? Why not turn it — here I was thinking consciously at last about something I had done unconsciously before — into what I now termed the concealed essay, in which personal anecdote was allowed gently to bring under observation thoughts of a more purely scientific nature?" The result was his classic, *The Immense Journey,* and other books, which not only gave him a place in American literature but enabled him to deal scientifically with contemporary life and to interpret it in a more popular, more appealing, and more effective manner.

And that's the inventive and imaginative way Jesus expects all of us to live and act in God's kingdom in the face of hunger, disease, economic tragedy, terrorism, war and the bomb, or anything else that threatens our existence.

Magic Mountain

For six days, Jesus had been engaged in an inner struggle, attempting to settle, once and for all, his decision to go to Jerusalem where, he knew, he would die. In a move not unique to the Jews when there was any religious critical question to be settled, Jesus took Peter, James, and John apart from the rest of the disciples and went to a "high mountain" for a retreat. He needed their company, comfort, and support as he was about to lay his life on the line. Was he doing the right thing? Had he interpreted the will of God for him correctly? Was he really God's Messiah and, if so, was this what God wanted him to do?

Do you remember what, according to Matthew, occurred at Caesarea Philippi just before the retreat? Jesus asked the disciples, "Who do people say that I am?" They said, "Some say John the Baptist, others say Elijah or Jeremiah, or one of the other prophets." "But who do *you* say that I am?" Jesus questioned more directly. Peter immediately spoke up and said, "You are the Christ, the Son of the living God." A breakthrough had come at long last; one of the disciples had perceived who he really was and, to him, Jesus said, "You are Peter, and on this Rock I will build my church." And then, once more, Jesus told them they were going to Jerusalem where all the things written about him by the prophets — relating to his death — would be accomplished. Peter got the message — "God forbid, Lord" — and that's possibly why Jesus took him along on the retreat, with James and John, who must have understood, too. They went to a nearby mountain, climbed up to a suitable spot for their retreat, and then the almost magical event took place.

An ordinary mountain became a magic mountain right before

their eyes. Jesus' face shone, much like Moses' did when he spent those forty days and nights on Mount Sinai and returned to the people with the stone tablets bearing the Ten Commandments. Even Jesus' clothing seemed as bright as a minor sun. "Maybe the enemies of Jesus were right, and maybe we were wrong in calling him the Christ," Peter and James and John might have reacted, "because he does great feats of magic. He's a great magician." To be great, as a magician, Jesus would have had to do better tricks of magic than others, as Doug Henning points out: "Better means creating the most wonder." Henning says that small illusions are "the poetry of magic, because (they) allow people to see the beauty of what we (magicians) do . . . Sure I can make big things vanish, but I want to do something that is so simple — with no boxes or curtains or anything — that it amazes people. I want to do something that even other magicians won't be able to figure out how I did it."

Actually, it was God who did the magic act on the mountain, and he needed no props beyond the natural surroundings and the four men. Even the best magicians need props of some kind to do magic tricks. Henning's latest tricks do, but he attempts to use simply what is at hand: "For one trick, I'm going to borrow three finger rings from members of the audience and link them together. For another, I'm going to take a piece of rope and have two people come on the stage and each take an end. I'm going to cut the rope and tie a knot in it near one end. Then, I'm going to take that knot and slide it from one end of the rope to the other. And when I'm done, I'm going to untie the rope and let the people take the two pieces back to their seats with them," apparently, to try to figure out how he did the trick, or simply to wonder about it and marvel at his ability to do magic.[52]

If the disciples were at all inclined to think that what was happening was an act of magic, they soon changed their minds, because two other figures appeared and, immediately, they knew who they were — Moses and Elijah. Suddenly they knew that they were seeing the glory of the Lord in a vision, and not simply a magic show on the mountain; that's why Peter spoke to Jesus and said, "Lord, it's good that we are here; if you wish, I will make three booths here, one for you, one for Moses and one for Elijah." He wanted to mark the spot and turn the place into a religious shrine, which he and the disciples and others might visit to worship the Lord their God. Perhaps Peter believed that God was going to take Jesus from the mountain, as he did Moses and Elijah centuries before. Do you remember how President Reagan insisted he had done the right thing after he visited the cemetery in Bitburg, West Germany, despite the fact that it contained the bodies of at least twenty-nine Nazi SS soldiers, and later, as if to offset the visit to Bitburg, made a pilgrimage to one of the concentration camps? His argument, supporting his contention that he had done a good deed, was based on what he learned about the manner in which the German people actually make pilgrimages to some of the death camps to keep alive the terrible memory in adults and make children realize how awful those camps were. Graphic and gruesome photographs and news stories of the atrocities, uncovered after the Allies liberated them, are posted in prominent places so no one would ever forget. "Let me build three booths here" was Peter's way of marking the spot of Jesus' Transfiguration so no one would ever forget.

Could it be that Peter overheard the conversation, which Luke reports in condensed form, in which they confirmed Jesus' fate and assured him God would see him through that terrible experience which he had to face? We'll never know but what we do know is, before Peter had gotten the words out of his mouth, another Voice spoke and rendered Peter, James, and John speechless and almost scared to death: "This is my beloved Son, with whom I am well pleased; listen to him." It was of critical importance that the disciples should fully understand not only that Jesus would die in Jerusalem, but also the significance of Jesus' death. He would rise again — on the third day — which might have been seen as a major miracle wrought by Christ, or the greatest feat of magic the world has ever witnessed. Death was going to be defeated, and they were going to see it happen; then, indeed, would they see and be prepared to tell the whole world about the glory of the Lord revealed in Jesus Christ. Once and for all, Christ would gain an eternal victory over death.

Death always seems so final, so permanent, as if there is nothing that can be done about it, especially when someone you love and admire dies. One of my pastors, John Manz, told about such an experience: "I suppose because all of us have received bad news over the phone there is something about its ringing at an odd hour which makes the heart beat just a little quicker. That happened in our house . . . I had the sense that something was wrong. The voice on the other end belonged to a college friend; 'Kent is dead,' she said. 'He drowned in Mexico.' I hadn't seen him for a long time. Lives which intersect unfold along different lines. Perhaps because he was a musician, a brilliant organist and treasured student of my father, we developed a friendship . . . What a strange feeling to once again be learning to talk about a friend in the past tense." John adds: "The friend who told me had buried her husband just a couple of years ago. He was just a young man who left behind two little children, one just an infant. She said, 'Of all people you would think I should be prepared and strong for this kind of thing. But I am not.' I found myself thinking that there must be some mistake. I caught myself nurturing the ghastly hope that maybe it was someone else. I half expected to hear in the retelling of that story that there was a way it would turn out all right after all. But the news was final, a prelude to a week which would take us to another cruel death and a cold cemetery unmoved by any amount of tears."[53] Did Peter, James, and John understand that Jesus was about to die and God would raise him up again?

Matthew doesn't tell us the answer to that. It was Jesus who spoke to the three disciples, saying, "Don't be afraid . . . Rise, and have no fear." They did just that, still, trembling a bit from the voice that had spoken to them and, in a way, affected a sort of coronation for Christ as King of Kings and Lord of Lords, on that very mountain. They knew they had seen the glory of the Lord and heard God's voice, and as glorious as the experience had been, it completely overwhelmed them. But Jesus knew Peter, and probably the other two, would get their voices back very soon and broadcast, to any who would listen, what took place on that particular mountain. At first they wanted to stay there, but I suspect that by the end of the story they couldn't wait to get down from those mountain heights and tell the other nine disciples, and anyone else they might encounter, about their experience — "You won't believe what happened up on that mountain. Let me tell you the story . . . " As they went down the mountain, Jesus said to them, "Tell no person the story of the vision, until the Son of man is raised from the dead."

Jesus wanted them to connect that mountain-top experience to his agony and death in the light of his resurrection. He wanted them to be able to tell the whole story so it would be properly told and understood by people, instead of being rejected or misinterpreted as some kind of an act of magic. And he wanted them to know what his death and resurrection meant — that death has been destroyed in this one man who accepted death on the cross and rose again on the third day. John Manz writes again about Jesus' death and his friend's death: "On its own terms death had met its match. Not even the devil could thwart the spotless life voluntarily laid down on behalf of those who knew all too well about paying with their life. And from this point the fabric of the grave has begun to unravel." He adds, "That for me is the deeper, more pressing reason for remembering my friend tonight as I hope you are remembering yours. It really has happened. Just for once what we mistakenly call the natural process has been reversed. Death hasn't been skipped. It wasn't circumvented. It has its moment. But in Jesus its victory has been snatched away. It's not allowed to claim the last word. The resurrection of our Lord is so strong it flavors all of our living and even our dying . . . The message of Easter is that hope really does lie on the other side of despair."[54] That's what Jesus wanted the disciples to be prepared to teach and preach after his resurrection and, I am certain, why he silenced them: "Tell no one this story until after my resurrection."

So, the Christmas cycle comes to an end and we begin Lent in three days. We have heard the wondrous story of the Cradle, his birth, and the prediction of his death and resurrection, the Cross event, and we look forward to the time he will return and all the world will know, as did the disciples at his Transfiguring, that he will rule and wear a God-given Crown. Crown him Lord of all!

Notes

1. *Omni,* in its December, 1984, issue, published Arthur C. Clarke's account of how he builds "a space-adventure story on a solid foundation of scientific fact." The pictorial article is simply called "2010 (Odysset Two)."

2. From a piece by columnist Jim Klobuchar in the *Minneapolis Star and Tribune,* October 28, 1984.

3. This article appeared in the *Minneapolis Star and Tribune* on May 30, 1985.

4. The Imprimatur Gallery is located in the old, but refurbished, main railroad station in St. Paul, Minnesota.

5. Descriptions of these two churches appear in *The Renewal of Liturgical Preaching* (Augsburg, 1967).

6. The thesis was written in 1948 for the master of sacred theology degree at the Lutheran Theological Seminary, Philadelphia, and was related to alcoholism in the parish.

7. The sermon, "Doing Evangelism," by Dr. James Burtness, was published in the Luther Northwestern Theological Seminary *Story,* Spring, 1985. In its entirety, it is a fine example of one type of a contemporary narrative sermon, although I have used only part of it as an illustration in my sermon.

8. Participants in a Preaching From Commitment seminar saw and discussed this film in conjunction with parish preaching.

9. John Lewis is a Baptist lay missionary pilot, who flies "mercy missions" in Zaire, Africa.

10. Morton Smith, *Jesus the Magician.* San Francisco: Harper and Row, 1978, p. vii.

11. "Henning concentrating on small wonders" was an article by Jeff Strickler in the *Minneapolis Star and Tribune,* May 31, 1985.

12. From John Masefield's *Saul Kane.*

13. Ray Bradbury, *The Stories of Ray Bradbury.* New York: Alfred A. Knopf, 1980, p. 692 f.

14. From Jeff Strickler's article on Doug Henning.

15. Ed Regis, Jr., in *Omni,* December, 1983, p. 122 f.

16. Author unknown.

17. From a chapel sermon published in the Luther Northwestern *Bell,* Fall, 1979.

18. As reported in the *Mineapolis Star and Tribune,* June, 1985.

19. From a Lutheran Social Service mailing in the summer, 1985.

20. A news article in the *Minneapolis Star and Tribune,* June 2, 1985.

21. Ray Bradbury, *The Stories of Ray Bradbury,* pp. xii, xiv.

22. Hymn number 50 in the *Service Book and Hymnal.* Minneapolis: Augsburg Publishing House (and others), 1958.

23. " 'Biloxi Blues' hits close to Simon's heart" was written by Samuel G. Freedman for the *New York Times,* and was published in the *Minneapolis Star and Tribune,* May 31, 1985.

24. Russell Baker, *Growing Up.* New York and Scarborough, Ontario: New America Library, Inc., 1983, p. 35.

25. Ellen Goodman's syndicated columns appear regularly in the *Minneapolis Star and Tribune.* This one was published in January, 1985.

26. The Associated Press released this story on June 10, 1985.

27. Loren Eiseley, *The Star Thrower.* New York: Times Books, 1978, p. 129 f.

28. Loren Eiseley, p. 138 of *The Star Thrower.*

29. The December, 1984, issue of *Omni* carried Michael Swanwick's short story, "Trojan Horse."

30. Gerard Sloyan, *Commentary on the New Lectionary*. New York: Paulist Press, 1975, p. 26.

31. Ray Bradbury, *The Martian Chronicles*. New York: Time Books, 1960.

32. See *Plastic Flowers in the Holy Water* (C.S.S., 1981) and *You are My Beloved* (Concordia, 1981) for other sermons on baptism (25).

33. *Time* called Ali Agca's 1985 trial "The Trial of the Century," June 10, 1985.

34. "Suspect in priest killing cleared to stand trial" was released by the Associated Press, June, 1985. The three murders occurred on February 7, 1985, in Onalaska, Wisconsin.

35. Associated Press published "Black leaders allege plot against Bishop Tutu, 13 other activists," June 13, 1985.

36. Another Associated Press story on June 13, 1985.

37. From an article by Alice Steinbach, originally published in the *Baltimore Sun,* May 27, 1984.

38. Nora Boustany published "Shiites rise to dominance from deprivation" in the *Washington Post,* June 14, 1985.

39. From an article in the *Minneapolis Star and Tribune.*

40. *Minneapolis Star and Tribune,* June 14, 1985.

41. Only the beginning of this story has been published, as yet.

42. An excerpt from a *Minneapolis Star and Tribune* story.

43. See p.270 f. of the *Service Book and Hymnal.*

44. This reaction to the film was written shortly after I saw it on TV.

45. *Minneapolis Star and Tribune,* June 10, 1985.

46. See Mary Sharpe's *A Guide to the Churches in Rome.* Philadelphia and New York: Chilton Books, 1966, for an interesting reference to Nero's presence at Tre Fontana when Paul was beheaded.

47. A story told in most of the biographies of Russell H. Conwell.

48. Loren Eiseley, *All the Strange Hours.* New York: Charles Scribner's Sons, 1975, p. 177 f.

49. "Free At Last" was preached by Paul Peterson in Gloria Dei Lutheran Church, St. Paul, October 28, 1984.

50. Romano Guardini, *The Saints in Daily Life.* Philadelphia and New York: Chilton Books, 1966, p. 55.

51. Eiseley, *All the Strange Hours,* pp. 182, 183.

52. From the previously quoted Strickler article about magician Doug Henning.

53. This is an excerpt from an Easter Evening, 1985, sermon which John Manz preached in Gloria Dei Lutheran Church, St. Paul, Minnesota.

54. From the same sermon.